DACIA

LOVE LETTERS

UNEDITED LETTERS
BY GABRIELE D'ANNUNZIO,
PRESENTED AS THEATRE

TRANSLATED BY THOMAS SIMPSON

FOLLOWED BY AN INTERVIEW WITH DACIA MARAINI
BY BRANKO GORJUP

GUERNICA

TORONTO·BUFFALO·CHICAGO·LANCASTER (U.K.)

2003

Francesca Valente, Guest Editor
Guernica Editions Inc.
P.O. Box 117, Station P, Toronto (ON), Canada M5S 2S6
2250 Military Road, Tonawanda, N.Y. 14150-6000 U.S.A.

Distributors:
University of Toronto Press Distribution,
5201 Dufferin Street, Toronto, (ON), Canada M3H 5T8
Gazelle Book Services, Falcon House, Queen Square,
Lancaster LA1 1RN U.K.
Independent Publishers Group,
814 N. Franklin Street, Chicago, Il. 60610 U.S.A.

First edition.
Printed in Canada.

Legal Deposit — First Quarter
National Library of Canada
Library of Congress Catalog Card Number: 2002113554
National Library of Canada Cataloguing in Publication
Maraini, Dacia
Love letters / Dacia Maraini, author ;
Thomas Simpson, translator.
(Drama series ; 23)
Play in Italian with English translation.
ISBN 1-55071-178-4
1. D'Annunzio, Gabriele, 1863-1938 – Correspondance.
2. Authors, Italian –19th century – Correspondence.
3. Authors, Italian – 20th century – Correspondence.
I. Simpson, Thomas. II. Title. III. Series.
PQ4873.A69L69 2002 856'.8 C2002-904864-8

CONTENTS

ACKNOWLEDGEMENTS

The author would like to thank the directors of the Istituti Italiani di Cultura who have been involved in the publication of *Love Letters:* Francesca Valente, Chicago; Annamaria Lelli, San Francisco; Guido Fink, Los Angeles; Carlo Coen, Toronto; Lidia Ramogida, Oslo; Paolo Giordano, President of Italidea, Chicago; Eileen Mackevich, President of the Chicago Humanities Festival; Thomas Simpson, Northwestern University; and Anna Fiore, Consolato Generale d'Italia Chicago.

This work was produced on the occasion of the XIII Chicago Humanities Festival. World Premiere: Istituto Italiano di Cultura, Chicago, November 9, 2002, with the participation of Dacia Maraini and Marisa Fabbri, featuring recorded music by Quartetto Paradiso from Avellino – Massimo Barone, Roberto De Caro, Fracesco Merone and Giovanni Venezia.

Mara enters with a box in her arms. She sits in a chair lighted by a standing lamp. She opens the box and begins to read the sheets.

MARA

"My dear Barbara: Yesterday I wrote you briefly. I didn't want to tell you how badly my migraines torture me. It was as though I couldn't see anymore. Your letter consoled me. I ate the violets, they perfumed my heart and seemed sweeter to me than any precious fruit. Then I thought about you all day, all day long, with unspeakable tenderness. I remembered the tiniest details of our lovemaking, sometimes feeling a peculiar pleasure and sometimes a suffocation of desire. *Addio*. I kiss your mouth. I desire you very much. Tell it to the original rose" (March 17, 1888).

Mara looks the sheet up and down.

Signed, Gabriele... Gabriele... Who is this?

She turns the letter in her hands.

"Dear Barbara..." Mamma, this love letter is addressed to you! You never told me you received love letters... When could you have met him? Where? How? ...I can't believe it... So, as you swept the steps, grumbling, you were nursing such a huge secret, so huge, Mamma, it's not possible...

Mara starts reading again.

"We've been apart for fifteen days, an entire century, my Barbara. Today is my birthday. My room is filled with flowers. Jonquils, narcissus, and hyacinths have such a strong perfume that I feel a little drunk. But today is grey, heavy, irritating, perhaps like the one that made you so restless yesterday. I shall think about you a lot today... I feel so languid. If you were here, I'd spend hours in your arms dreaming and making you caress me like a lazy, drowsy cat. What would I give for you to make an apparition today among these flowers! Your mouth must be burning like a flame and your breath must be as perfumed as the roses you have in your heart. *Addio*, gentle Barbarella. I love you and call out for you, Gabriele."

Mara stops to reflect, ever more surprised and stunned.

He loved you so much! But where could you hide such a passionate lover so that neither I nor Father ever found out? Motherhood, the house... I laugh, I laugh at anyone who presumes that a woman in love should resign herself, that she should take her sweet bones and lock them in a tomb, maybe with an engraved stone: Here lies a mother who could have loved but didn't, out of her spirit of sacrifice! It's too funny, too funny...

Mara begins to read again.

"I wrote you this morning while oppressed by an atrocious sadness. To overcome it I went out and walked down to the sea. At the rotonda at Castellammare I saw a little girl who had your mouth and your eyes and, in certain movements, your childlike expression. What a strange similarity! I still haven't seen your portrait from that time, but I think you must have looked like that. Especially the mouth; oh, that mouth! That little girl, barely four years old, is called Elvezia. I gave her many kisses on her face, her eyes, her hair. She looked at me stupefied, almost afraid.

I'm very ill. My nerves are so shaken I can write only with effort. My hand shakes and trembles like that of a paralytic. *Addio*, good Barbarella. I kiss you all over. Can you still feel my burning sweet tunic of kisses on your breasts? There were one hundred and sixty, remember? I write with a spirit perfumed with love, melancholy, and jasmine, while in the room next door my friend plays the clarinet..."

We hear the sound of a clarinet. Mara kisses the letter and gazes dreamily into the emptiness.

Such an insignificant little mother. A mother you wouldn't give a penny for... Mamma, those egg-colored house slippers you put on as soon as you got home so as not to dirty the floor. You shuffled them along the ground like snails. I watched your clumsy walk and thought: poor, poor mamma, she never got anything from life. I saw you as yellowish as those slippers. I wanted to kiss those minuscule feet. But I didn't dare. Because little and straw-colored as you were, you were still very severe with me and wouldn't have stood for such intimacy. Never. But in fact you were hiding an incommensurable treasure!"

Mara begins reading again.

"Yesterday I spent the whole day preparing my room in the enchanted castle. It was sad but sweet work. Your spirit was present. Everything spoke to me of you. If only you could see the 'pillow of caresses' in the light of day! The signs of love he has borne are evident... The pale silk flowers have grown shiny and a bit worn at the edges. All the fabric has a peculiar odor, extremely subtle but perceptible to my nostrils, expert at aspiring the most hidden waves of aroma.

Do you remember the high cries of our supreme ecstasy? And the drowsing afterwards, the ineffable sweetness of profound weariness of the flesh? Do you remember everything?

I have hung the curtains and the tapestries on the wall. I await you. Yesterday when I finished I stretched out on the divan with my head on the magic pillow and dreamed for a long time. Between the green curtains, rustled by the wind, appeared the blue sea, peopled by red sails.

I dreamed a less sad life, a labor less solitary... Oh, to feel the resonant house rejoice in your song..."

Mara is surprised.

Mamma, you even sang! While I've never heard your voice except in stern, sad rebuke. You twisted your mouth with an angry, dark little twitch. You sang!

Mara reads.

"To feel myself suddenly enwrap your throat and kiss the nape of your neck... to rest on your nude body with its softness of the softest velvets and the perfume of an unknown fruit!"

Mara comments.

"The softest of velvets," you Mamma, who were a

piece of iron. With those hard, aching little hands you used to cut onions, make batter from flour, drag the hot iron over Father's shirts, with those hands you caressed the body of a man dying of love for you, hiding in secret rooms, and then you came back home and took up cleaning, sewing, ironing… It isn't possible.

Mara reads.

"Yesterday, suddenly, the desire for you seized me with a dolorous vehemence. It was almost noon. I had bathed in the sea and I was naked in the sun on the beach. There was a delicious caress of the sea air mixed with the smell of the rays that wrapped me in a golden net.

I closed my eyes and lost myself in contemplation of you. All at once the exquisitely soft fresh caress of the air on my warm body gave me a live image of the pleasure of once upon a time. I felt your mouth, your sucking mouth, my only ecstasy, my slow death coming close, the sweet spasm of my soul" (July 14, 1888).

Mara comments.

What sumptuous language, what serpentine grace! Sensuality so soft but lucid at the same time! What a man, Mamma! Where did you find a man so passionate and so good at speaking his passion! And where was I, Mamma, while you were loving him? Why didn't you let me meet him?

Mara reads.

"As soon as I woke this morning I looked at my body scorched by the sun. The skin was peeling from my entire bust, but especially from the shoulders, where you used to rest your head. I carefully peeled away the strips of skin and I thought, perhaps in those dead flakes there was still the sign of your cheek and your kisses. I shed my first layer of skin like a serpent. What ecstasy that empty skin contained!

I feel your mouth on my cheeks and throat. It opens and closes softly sliding, caressing and tempting. When you kissed me, then I was lost!"

Mara comments.

O God, great God, how could such a hurricane of the senses have passed through our poor rooms without our becoming conscious of it! Now I understand the meaning of certain of your departures, Mamma. You said you were going out to look for some fabric for sewing. You said you were going to the seamstress. And you disappeared for two or three hours. Then you came back modestly, always shut up in your black clothes, buttoned up to the throat, your face without makeup, hair pulled back onto the nape of your neck. Who could imagine?... Mamma, I'm asking you: Who were you? Who did I have for a mother? An astute deceiver? A suffering and secret lover of mystery? A cynical impostor? An unconscious madwoman? A beautiful fairy with deep blue hair? I don't know, honestly, I don't know anymore...

Clarinet. Mara reads.

"Yesterday, coming back to my room I noticed your pastel portrait was gone. Might Carmelo have spirited it away, perhaps for a laugh? I went up to the Convent, saw Carmelo, and began speaking bitter words to him, I don't know why. Anger invaded me bit by bit. I ended up offending him mortally, leaving him no escape. I couldn't see anymore, I no longer knew what I was doing and saying. Who knows what physiological reasons made me give in to that ferocious impulse?

My madness lasted for some time. I stayed in bed all day with a violent fever. I feel better now and think back on this strange phenomenon with great sadness. Could man perhaps be necessarily, inevitably subject to sudden, inexplicable re-apparitions of primitive bestiality?

Kiss my forehead, my face, my mouth, caress me, tell me many sweet sisterly things. Forgive me for not writing yesterday, and for writing so poorly today. I love you endlessly. And you?"

Mamma, remember when you came to wake me up in the morning for school? You threw the windows open. I would scream: Wait a minute, Mamma, the light's too bright, it's blinding me. But you didn't care. You banged the shutters, *bang bang*, then you came over and pulled the sheets off my bed with a spartan gesture. How I hated you!

Mara reads again.

"It has been a terrible night. I never closed my eyes; such horrible pain. I took the wrong dose of a medicine; I swallowed a great quantity of tartaric acid thinking I was taking a tranquilizer. The fever came back. I'm better now, but my nerves are so irritated and weak that I tremble all over at the least sound. My pulse beats out of order; sometimes I can't find it at all, sometimes it's so rapid and strong that the noise seems to fill the room.

I have an unspeakable desire for your company. I don't know what I'd give to have you here, to read your eyes, to return to the safety of your love. Doubt is such anguish when the spirit is so thin and clear, vulnerable to the abuse of the dreams it imagines seeing and hearing.

Addio, love me and write me. The sky is veiled and the sea is swollen, half mud-colored and half terribly green. I shall die of melancholy before evening, I'm sure of it. Your Gabriele."

If you had pronounced this name, Gabriele, even once, Mamma, even one time. The name of an archangel furious with love... How could you preserve it intact and still in your mouth? Didn't you ever want to spit it all out? Didn't it leap on your tongue? Didn't it slither through your lips like an impudent snake? Oh, that clarinet that slips from the dark rooms of epistolary memory!

Clarinet. Mara reads again.

October 9. "This morning I took a long ride. Such a sudden cold! During the night the great mother, Majella, had covered herself with snow; the wind at sunset blew icy and strong. I returned to the Convent where I stay at about noon. Guess what strange thing! I had your barbaric portrait with me."

To herself.

Barbaric portrait? Could it be the one I did for you when I was thirteen? One green eye, one black one, a canary-colored nose, lilac lips, hair brick red. Oh Mamma, I was so proud of my painting! Without meaning to I'd made a barbaric portrait. A barbaric portrait!

Clarinet. Mara reads.

"You lose a lot in your photos, my Barbara. The image I have of you 'at the peak of my thoughts' is more effulgent, more beautiful, more vital, more loving, more desirable. With your barbaric portrait, I'll tell you, I've always had the temptation to cut out an eye to put in an antique locket my mother sent me. I resist, I resist, but I'll end up cutting out your eye. Forgive me.

I can't stand it anymore. Do you hear me? Your desires and your melancholy? I am in fury! At night I thrash in the bed and let out such strange cries in my sleep that I terrify whoever sleeps in the room next to mine. Cold baths help. I look at myself in the mirror: my eyes shine, almost flame, like some-one seized by dementia, by delirium; voracious eyes. You'll regret your kisses, you know which ones I mean. Let's speak of something else because I'm trembling as though I had tertian fever.

No caress, ah, no caress will be enough to satisfy my desire when I have you again. It feels as though to have enough of you I should drink you devour you put all of you inside me or enter completely inside of you. You choose!

Can you feel me trembling? My teeth are chat-tering like that first time when you became afraid in that miserable dark room. *Addio. Addio. Addio.* I feel I'm dying. I swear Barbara, I feel I'm dying, Gabriele."

To herself.

An unknown woman in the rooms of a too-well-known house. A gentle phantom, silent, who washes, sweeps, scrubs, irons, and carries inside herself a gigantic secret that never ever shows through to the eyes of her family. Mamma, you're a phenomenon! "No caress, no caress will be enough to satisfy my desire when I have you again..." It's so well said! "Language," Mamma, "reveals the body of the writer." So said my professor, Attanasio Ghirelli, and he was right. Poor Ghirelli, with his grimy little scarves, fingers yellow with nicotine, his grey moustache and his eyes... the eyes of a sad dog, perennially teary and melancholy...

Mara Giannini, outlived Gilberto Giannini, and outlived...? Outlived, no, professor, my mother is alive, she's alive and she scurries like a mouse, always rushing, always rushing... digging underground burrows that I thought made of family devotion but instead no, they were erotic passion, erotic passion, Professor Giannini!

Mara reads again.

"My jealousy, the jasmine spoke tender secrets while the black marks on the white paper told me things I still don't understand. I saved the perfume and didn't want to think anymore about the rest.

I shall write you again with my spirit perfumed with jasmine as I listen distractedly to the sound of the clarinet..."

Clarinet. Mara reads.

"Last night I had the happiness of dreaming always of you. At dawn I dreamed you so lusciously that I swooned. My bed is covered with that little red damask cover bordered with yellow that was at the head of our immense hidden bridal bed of one night only. What strange spectacles that damask has enjoyed! It's full of evocations. Perhaps the perfidiously sweet dreams come to me from that bed.

I can't bear to be far from you. In the evening

I regret you, at night I regret you, in the morning I regret you... I regret you every hour, every minute, every moment. When I get up, certain details of my toilette make me heave deep sighs. Do you smile?

Right now they are bringing me a cup of coffee, a common little coffee. Oh, that huge deep black fuming coffee you poured for me with such a gentle gesture... I drink a sip and I send you an infinite kiss. Spirit, my spirit..."

Mara reflects.

He was jealous, this guy... Jealous, Mamma, but of whom? Of me, right? Of me, certainly. He must have known that your hands rested on my body, patient and gentle, and not on his, as he would have wanted. He must have known that you bent over me in the morning and your sweet breath fell onto my eyelids still closed, he must have known about those big cups of steaming coffee you made for me and not for him. My father? I really don't think he could have been jealous of Father.

You're so funny, Mamma. You make such grimaces, even when dead, that I really can't help laughing. But do you remember how you slept together in the same bed, you and Father, as though the Sahara stretched between you; one curled up at the extreme eastern border and the other at the extreme west. Two separate continents, two bodies living right next to each other that never met. Never.

I never saw Father kiss you, not even once. Not even when I was little and you were young and fresh. I never saw him take your hand, or say an affectionate word to you. He came and went with those dark, melancholy eyes of his, the grim face, the mouth so sealed that it would have needed a special key to open it, and it seemed no one in the family ever had it.

I asked myself then why you got married, Mamma? Why? But yes, I know: you were pregnant with me. You confessed it to me once, almost without wanting to. Your mouth half-closed, Mamma, your eyes down... You know, there's nothing to be ashamed of. I know how these things happen... "We snuck off to the movies because, you know, in our town it wasn't allowed for a girl and a boy..." Mamma, you trembled while you told me about that night, like you had a fever...

"We snuck off to the movies. And after the movies, he squeezed me hard on the church wall and then... then I found myself pregnant and I didn't even know it." *Gloria in excelsis dei!*

It took so much for that confession to come out! You waited centuries. Only when I became twenty-one did you feel you had the right, or maybe the duty, to tell me the story of the movies and the embrace... And how old were you, Mamma, when you got pregnant? Nineteen? Almost the same as me. I had turned twenty-one the month before and I was still a virgin, virgin as a wild goat... I didn't think about love, I was afraid, a foolish fear, terrible. And it was you, really you Mamma, who inculcated that fear in me. You trembled, I trembled. You covered yourself, I covered myself. You escaped, I escaped. Without knowing anything, without even imagining that behind that fleeing there was another love, another desire, the real one. Mamma, you shouldn't have done this to me! While you talked to me about homework, schoolteachers, shoes, cutlets, in your heart you

were listening to Gabriele's clarinet! Damned ferocious motherhood!

Clarinet. Mara reads.

"When I think that the main cause of your pain and
your family aggravation is me, an unspeakable
regret stabs me and I wish you knew all my passion
for you, to forgive me the damage. Are you sure
that my love is worth yours, is worth your pain?
Are you certain, secure, profoundly conscious of
it? You will never imagine the dismay I have in my
soul. My greatest torment is the implacable lucidity
of this fantastic vision. I see you contorted in
excess, I see your features distort and turn livid,
your eyes spinning desperately under lids red with
crying... No matter how hard I try I cannot chase
away the horrid vision. Then I hear you calling me.
I have the sound of your voice in my ears, a hoarse
lamenting sound like someone calling for help
without any hope for help..."

Mara comments.

He made you suffer, Mamma, this archangel
Gabriele, he wrung you out like a rag, he squeezed
your throat with those seductive hands. How could
you forgive him? He knew that you suffered, he
knew your distorted, livid features... Exactly, exactly... How many times did I come home from
school to find you collapsed on the kitchen table
with your face twisted in a terrible grimace of
suffering? Mamma, what's the matter? Are you
sick? No, Mara, I'm fine, go to your room, do your
homework, shall I make you some coffee? Yes,
Mamma, with lots of ice. And I flew away to my
books, with my big glass of coffee with ice, without

dwelling on your reticence, your pain, so effort-fully withheld. But would you have spoken if I had said: Talk? Would you have told me about this Gabriele who tortured your body in secret? Mamma, tell me, would you have spoken with your little froggy, as you called me sometimes? Your stupid little froggy who lived with you so long and never understood anything. I went off to study Tacitus. Like an idiot, and I sipped my coffee with little sips, even when it melted down to ice and water. Mamma, why did you betray me like this? I wasn't your husband, I could have been your friend. Why didn't you tell me a single word? And now that you're dead you dump this avalanche of words of love and desire on me. How could you do it? How can you?

Clarinet. Mara reads.

"I think, think, think sharply and the sharpness of the thought gives me an inhuman spasm. Some-times I feel a furious mania to tear from my aching temples this impalpable thing, stronger and more inflexible than a stinger. Breathing is an unbearable effort and the beating in my veins aggravates me like the pounding of a hammer I'm condemned to listen to. Is this love? Oh no. This is a sort of prodigious disease that flowers only in my being, it becomes my joy and my agony... I shall never ever have inner peace and inner security. I shall never be satisfied except on one sole condition: by ab-sorbing all all of your being and becoming one single being with you, living your life, thinking your thoughts... I wish at least that your senses were closed to any sensation that didn't come to you from me..."

Mara comments.

What demands, what possessiveness! How could he think that she would cancel me from her life? How could he demand that she feel nothing, nothing beyond her desire for him! What arrogance, my Gabriele, I must tell you, my mother was right not to accept your invitation... You deny having obsessed her with the demand to leave everything, husband, daughter and house, to come with you? Can you deny it? But she, she always refused. That's what cursed you, admit it... You couldn't tolerate her devotion to her family, despite the love, despite the delirium of her senses. Family, dear Gabriele, is the only reality that counts, the only one, remember that... But what am I saying? Me, the one who hated that family? ...Family, family, that viscid and indecipherable thing that slithers, spreads out, and disappears to suddenly reappear like a dragon hungry for caresses... But still, but still, no matter how divided, torn, chopped off, tortured, my mother stayed faithful to the family. Nothing can be done. That's the way it is, the way it is...

Clarinet. Mara reads.

"I still don't understand, I do not understand your affection for that man and I cannot fight off an angry sensation that also goes partly against you. So as not to torment you I don't write you my thoughts. They are bitter and very dark. I feel that my tenderness has been poisoned for some time now. I think it's better if you don't see me again. Don't come back to me if you'd rather spare yourself useless suffering. I am not good now. My soul loves you and prostrates itself and my thought bites you and stains you. And the conflict always starts over again, it will never end. Suffering, atrocious suffering comes back... I want to see you, speak to you, caress you. I love you like never before... but spare me the sight of your bruises. I cannot think about them without horror and anger. It feels that if I saw your flesh damaged by those hands my heart would shatter..."

Mara reflects.

Maybe your husband understood. That's why he raised his hands against you, is that it, Mamma? A scream in the night. I still get gooseflesh. I am running and you are telling me: It's nothing, nothing, my Mara. But I saw the nightshirt torn and those black marks on your neck. He tried to strangle you, say it, he tried to kill you, say it! ...That pacific, mute man, that grey methodical man, had he found a letter? I will never know. I will never know.

The caretaker said she set her watch by my father. Seven on the dot, not a second after, not a second before: lawyer Gianni Giannini, pearl-grey suit, silver grey hair, mouse grey briefcase, lead grey moustache shined with a touch of olive oil stolen from the kitchen – the only extravagance in his perfectly anonymous appearance – the lawyer Gianni Giannini left home with a regular step, got into his iron grey Polo, turned the key and waited with faithful grey patience for the motor to warm up. As he waited he lit a cigarette from which rose grey smoke soft and curly as a cloud, and when the motor had warmed up, he pressed the accelerator, arms tense on the wheel, to go live his day as completely regulated by grey norms as wet asphalt.

It's very strange that he could understand something about my mother's secrets. His life was not prepared for surprises of any kind. Unpredictable happenings were excluded from his days, each one accurately prepared beforehand, without any possibility of eruption of the unexpected.

Only with me once in a while did he permit himself a transgression: Would you like some ice cream, Marina? He was the only one who called me Marina. "My sweet-smelling Marina," he said, and he took my hand. Father, can we go to the movies? Father, can we go skating? Yes, baby, on Sunday. I want to go today. Go with your mamma. But Mamma had too much to do. Papà, please... His mouth folded in a bitter, reproachful smile. He didn't approve of your way of raising me, so spartan and severe, Mamma, he didn't approve of anything at all.

And Gabriele would have been jealous of a man like that? Jealous of that bed, of that body? A husband is a husband, my baby... How can you escape it? You couldn't resist laughing. You put your hand over your mouth. Because you'd been trained that way. Like a true peasant.

Clarinet. Mara reads.

"Everything here is violence, spasm, excess. Where are my delicacies? Where are my exquisite, complicated melancholies? Where are the profound and tortuous afflictions in which my spirit lost itself as in inextricable labyrinths?

You departed, you departed before I could see you and cover your face with kisses! Around eleven as though by instinct I turned over. Your husband came in with two friends. I was seized with a

convulsion of pain so strong, I had to get up shortly
after and go out.

But I doubt. My spirit is hostile to you today. I
am full of compressed anger. I will go out in a while
and into the sea. The waves are cheerful and strong.
Addio. I won't write anymore so as not to say
terribly harsh things to you. *Addio*. Do you love
me? Or do you only write of love out of habit and
pity? Are you faithful? What are you thinking?
What are you doing? I suffer. I have the right to
interrogate you this way. I doubt, I doubt, I doubt.
I am demented..."

Mara reflects.

I swear that my mother was faithful, totally faithful... how can you doubt her good faith? How can
you think of saying "terribly harsh things" to a
woman who suffers, who writhes, who lacerates
herself in the pain of having to divide herself
between... But are you really so sure, Mara? Are
you really sure your mother was faithful? To
whom? If she always lied to you? If she lied to her
husband for years! She lied to you, innocent, with
the shrewdness of a secret, nocturnal fox; she could
have lied just as well to him, to her lover.

Clarinet. Mara reads.

"Where are you? Beyond what lands? Beyond what
seas? I pass the hours in inertia, thinking. This
room of mine has become as funereal as an underground chapel. Sometimes I see myself stretched
out in a coffin; I contemplate myself in the immo-
bility of death with an imperturbable lucidity..."

Mara reads.

"The sparrows twitter passing and re-passing in flocks like black arrows in the pallid rectangle cut by the balcony. What do I lack? What is the defect in my moral organism? What is the cause of my impotence? I have a burning longing to live, to unfold in rhythm all my strength, to feel myself complete and in harmony. But instead every day I perish secretly, every day life flees from me through innumerable invisible passageways. All my strength serves for nothing but to drag with immense effort a few grains of dust which my imagination gives the weight of gigantic millstones..."

Mara reflects.

But where does all this unhappiness come from? It wasn't her unhappiness but his... What restlessness! What irremediable dissatisfaction! But why? But in fact I recognize that dissatisfaction... It seems to me something of mine... How often do I ask myself the same questions...? And if I were... if I were the daughter of that man? To be born from love, no matter how secret, disordered, clandestine, unhappy, will be more propitious than to be born from daily habit and indifference!

Clarinet. Mara reads.

"There is on earth only one lasting rapture: the security of possessing another creature, the absolute, indestructible security. I seek this rapture. I want to be able to say: my lover, near or far, does not live except in thoughts of me. She is joyously submissive to my every desire, my will is her only law. If I ceased to love her, she would die...

It is a soft time of day, discreet, propitious for delicate sensualities. Oh, if only you were here with

me! I shall sleep once more alone. If you could only
see this bed! It is a rustic bed, a monumental altar
to Imeneus, wide as a threshing floor, deep as the
sleep of the Just. It's the Thalamus of Thalamuses.
The mattresses contain the wool of an entire herd
and the pallet contains the leaves of an entire field
of corn…"

Mara to herself.

"A soft time of day, discreet, propitious for delicate
sensualities" …This man, who I have already cho-
sen as my father, makes me see things as though
they were right before my eyes. He sculpts words
and though they're made of stone he makes them
airy and precious… extremely sweet. Decidedly,
Mamma, I hope you conceived me in that bed, on
those mattresses that contained the wool of an
entire herd…

Clarinet. Mara continues reading.

"I know that love is the greatest of all human
sorrows because it is the supreme effort that man
undertakes to escape from the solitude of his inner
being; an effort that, like all the others, is useless.
But just the same I reach out to love with invincible
zeal. I know well that love, being a phenomenon,
is the most fleeting figure, that which transforms
continually. But it's precisely that I aspire to, to
the perpetuity of love, a love that fills up an
entire existence. I also know that the fragility of
woman is incurable. But I cannot renounce the
hope that my woman be constant and faithful
until death…"

Mara comments.

He knows himself, he analyzes himself... with such acuity! Gabriele, my Gabriele, even from far away, even ignorant of what you're made of, if through my poor little unlucky maternal mother, if today I could fall in love with you... But, a portrait of him, a portrait of the archangel, Mamma, is it possible you didn't save one?

Digging around in the box.

Not a photograph, not a drawing, nothing.

Clarinet. Mara reads.

"With these attitudes, I remain useless and idle... Having begun to doubt myself, little by little I come to doubt everything. Having begun to suffer for myself, little by little I've begun to suffer for every-thing. I feel myself crushed by universal stupidity... Sometimes a thought occupies me, a single one, assiduous: the thought of death. In those moments every impression passes over my soul like a drop of water on a hot griddle, either dancing around or dissolving. I have pity on myself, understand?, and I am aware of the voluptuousness of compassion; a mysterious sadness that I dwell on.

There, now perhaps you know me better and know who you're dealing with, my Barbara. I'm that man with the invincible hereditary libido that takes pleasure, amidst the most fragrant delicacies, in calling his lover his sister, greedy for spiritual communion."

Clarinet. Mara reads.

"And yet this woman has belonged to others before me, I tell myself, I tell you. She has lain with another man, she has slept with another man in the same bed, on the same pillow... I repeat this to myself. In all women there is singularly alive a kind of physical memory, the memory of sensation. Do you remember the sensations you had from him? You cannot not remember... Can you have forgotten the man who violated you? What did you feel under the caress of your husband?"

Mara comments.

The caress of your husband? Only the wildest fantasy could go digging for a gesture where there was only emptiness. . . But how to content such a desire to possess? Nothing could have satisfied him, nothing in the world...

Clarinet. Mara reads.

"I would have wanted you to say to me: Here, take me as a virgin. I have known no ecstasy. I would have wanted to hear this from your lips. Even though I know that you transformed yourself in imitation of me, having taken on my thoughts, my judgments, my tastes, my distastes, my predilec-tions, my melancholies, everything that gives a spirit a special stamp, a character... But before, dear love, before we met, among what humiliating contacts did you spend those distant hours? This is what obsesses me, this is what I cannot tolerate... I think over those times I watched you set off to return to the house of your husband, to the house of a man totally unknown to me, to the vulgarity and meanness of bourgeois life, in the midst of which you were born and grew like a rare plant in a garden of common ones. Have you never hidden anything from me? Have you never deceived me? Have you always been able to escape from your husband's desire on the pretext of sickness? Always? Can you swear it?"

Mara comments.

Always, I can swear it!

Clarinet. Mara reads.

"Watching you sleep, delicate, complicated creature, closed in the mystery of sleep, you seemed to radiate from every pore an occult fascination of incredible intensity...and I felt once again deep inside myself a vague impulse of instinctive terror.

I cannot deflect, I cannot repress this mad insurrection of fear, suspicion, doubt...I wish I could scream at you: I don't love you anymore, it's all over, the flame is extinguished."

Mara reads.

"You become every day more puerile in your actions, your tastes, your desires. Nothing runs between us but reactions of refined sensuality. Even in the pleasures of love you carry that studiousness and slowness with which you taste your favorite fruits, with which you prolong any other little delicacy, demonstrating your desire to live for nothing else, placing every attention in cultivating and decorating your and my sensations. Your pauses of silence and stillness come only from muscular fatigue..."

Clarinet. Mara reads.

"To destroy to possess; those who seek the Absolute in love have no other powers...If only I possessed true faith, that faith that permitted Saint Theresa really to see God in the host! Where,

where to find the secret of my unhappiness and my weakness!

"Who will kill desire? My love! In the sacred dawn of time, in an exquisite garden, I saw the first man, solitary and sad, draw to him his first companion. And in a short time this became the scourge of the world, scattering everywhere pain and death. But the sin of ecstasy seems more fierce to me, more shattering. No other intoxication but that of frenetic embrace seems equal to me to that to which the martyrs of the primitive Church abandoned themselves in their prisons, awaiting their torture."

Clarinet. Mara reads.

"Do I seem cruel to you, my soul? But I see a destructive aspect in you as well, the more obvious the stronger your orgasm under my caresses... In the darkness of night arises the terrifying, gorgon-like image of the woman who appears to me, her eyes half-lidded, convulsing in spasms or inert in extreme swooning...Like that time you pulled out the pin that held the carnation in your hair and put it between your teeth. Then slowly you opened your fist, took the imprisoned butterfly by its wings and prepared to stab it through. What cruelty, I said to you, how cruel you are! But you smiled, intent on your work, while the little victim beat its already faded wings. Your eyes were sparkling! You are a taciturn and sad woman who nurses inside herself the sacred evil, the astral disease; you are the covetous, convulsive lover whose ardor is sometimes almost fearful, whose lust sometimes seems like lugubrious agony..."

Mara thinks.

Astral disease... covetous, convulsive lover... but why, why this rebellion of a body in love? What had happened? Why?

Mara reads.

"The flaccid, oppressed, hesitant, feeble man I am leant his ear to a great poet philosopher. I listened to the new voice that fends off with bitter sarcasm the weakness, the irritability, the morbid sensibility, the cult of pity, the gospel of renunciation, the need to believe, the need to humiliate oneself, the need to redeem oneself, in effect all the most dubious spiritual needs of our time, all the laughable and miserable effeminacy of the old European soul, all the monstrous re-flowerings of Christian pestilence in the decrepit races.

The solitary man, the contemplative, the inert spectator that I am, leant his ear with strange anxiety to that voice that affirms life, that considers pain a discipline of the strong, that repudiates every faith and especially the faith in Morality, that proclaims the justice of inequality, who exalts the terrible energy, the feeling of power, the instinct for struggle and domination, the excess of generative, fertilizing forces, all the virtues of Dionysiac man, the conqueror, the destroyer, the creator."

Mara thinks.

He has stopped talking about love. His discourse has become embittered, scornful... He was sweet when asking for kisses, assurances. But now his letters have become dark, ferocious. Where did all that ardor go?

Mara reads.

"I can aspire to nothing but to an ending. And to bring an end to all dreams I must do nothing but dream to no longer wish to dream.

Is there not perhaps a need to give? Does receiving not perhaps equal having pity?

Between me and the other, my dear Spirit, there is nothing but pure friendship. I would have wanted you to read the other letters as well to convince yourself of my innocence. In that little note you read one word wrong. You must not speak of *partage,* there is no *partage.* She is no more than a friend and I shall tell you what kind of friend. And she knew about you and I spoke to her about you. Her gift of the dagger was for Christmas and I wrote the date on the grass. But since I knew you to be extraordinarily suspicious, I tried to keep you from reading it. I beg you, comprehend me. I want you to always be the good, the noble love, the sublime lover who can pardon yet another time, even while certain of my guilt. You know how much I love you and that I prefer you to any other creature on earth. You are the only one, now and forever" (letter April 14, 1892).

Mara thinks.

How could you bear all this torment? This tempest of lying words? ...You hid yourself, you hid yourself, retreating like a snail into its shell, your pain. And I, who never suspected anything!

Clarinet. Mara reads.

"How your little letter hurts me! When I'm upset, I bend to you, with profound trepidation, hoping to hear a good, consoling word, because I know you strong and straight, sympathetic and understanding.

Forgive me if I didn't know how to take you, forgive me if I didn't know how to lighten your pain, forgive me if I didn't know how to be the good, courageous brother you deserved. But how your little farewell letter hurts me. After four years of love and intimacy, I still open one of your letters with trembling fingers and I still feel a knot in my throat.

Forgive me, forgive me the doubts and the offensive certainties. I am not the one who doubts; it is someone inside me, a sick and evil being who drugs me with turbid vapors and takes away my reason.

Addio. Addio. Pray for me. Think of me and love me. I kiss you on the mouth: your Gabriele" (letter June 14, 1892).

Mara comments.

How can you bear the agony of a separation that you insisted on... because that's the way it is, isn't it? You're the one who wanted it, you're the one who sent the farewell letter. But I understand you, I understand you with all my heart, I understand you, Mamma. I know you were right to abandon him before he could abandon you with impatience. Your pride saved you. But is it right to say it saved you?

The letters are finished. Your story concluded rapidly. Four years of glory that you carried to the tomb with elegant stubbornness, with ferocious jealousy... If you had spoken about it with me... don't you believe I would have understood? Mamma, answer me, don't you believe I would have understood?

But here's another page. A page inside an envelope...

She takes the letter, observes it.

Another letter of regret? A letter of excuses? But what's the use by now? The pain has consumed itself.

She opens the letter. Reads.

"Dear Barbara, your perfumed letter has conquered me. I had answered you no, that one cannot sell one's own memories, or at least one cannot sell them to someone driven by fetishistic impulses, as yours seem to me. But then, rereading your delicate and dolorous missive, I thought over your proposal and came to a gentler counsel. What wrong is there is consenting to a small contract between two consenting adults who have in common a propensity for dreams and words of love? I apologize for my earlier no that must certainly have wounded you. But now here I am, with hat in hand and contrite face. I don't know whether it was the perfume in your letter that with subtle persistence penetrated my nostrils, or whether it was your gentle, humble, and at the same time passionate words that made me change my mind. But do you know that you have something else of the other Barbara, beyond her name? Do you know that your devoted persistence brought to mind another devoted persistence, one very dear and familiar to me? I am willing to bet that you are also gifted with light, nervous hands... I'm willing to bet that your hair is also thick and soft and invites lips to rest on it... Have I guessed? I would almost beg you to meet me. I am a secret and discreet visitor... But I don't want to disturb you... I know you have a husband and a daughter... I leave you wholly and completely to these sacred affections...

Rather, you have offered me five hundred *lire* for my letters to Barbara, which she herself returned to me at the moment of our parting... As I told you, I consent, on condition these letters remain in your home, that they not be published, so that she to whom they were directed never learn that I have ceded them to you...

The fact is that I find myself in an awkward moment in which even that little money could determine my future. I propose a thousand *lire* and the letters will be yours. Do you consent? If you can send me a voucher by telegraph, I will send you the letters immediately. You certainly know that in a few years they will be worth three times as much. And you will be able to resell them easily.

Farewell, dear Barbarina... that name, as you know, is dear to me, gravid with sumptuous, tender memories... that ghostly name, shadow of a distant, terribly powerful love... that name summons in memory innocent, charming gestures... I feel in you the repetition of a sacred votive offering; you, simulacrum of the lost and distant loving Barbara, you offer me a perfumed, adulterous breast to rest my weary, too-loving head. . .

Write me again, dear perfumed phantasm. Your affectionate words are ambrosia to me... and don't forget the telegram. The address is: Gabriele D'Annunzio, care of Micchetti, Lungomare Garibaldi, Francavilla, Abruzzo. Yours, Gabriele D'Annunzio."

Shocked, Mara lets the letter fall. Pause of surprise.

With a thousand *lire*, Mamma, with a thousand *lire* you have deceived me, swindled me, seduced me, run me around, cheered me up, made me melancholy, deluded me, amused me, made me suffer, defrauded me, conned me, entrapped me... with a thousand *lire*, you have made me suffer and exult. With a thousand *lire*... just a thousand *lire*... that... that in those days, however, I know you're right, in the days of your youth, were a lot, a whole lot.

Sing-songing.

If I could have a thousand *lire* a month... Who knows how much you suffered to set them aside, *lira* by *lira*... crumb by crumb... How could you manage, you without a coin to your name, my industrious little ant... But dreams must be paid for, and you, the good housewife, you bought them all by yourself with savings, setting aside a little here and there, stealing a bit of the shopping money, my poor mother, you paid for your private dream, your private dream, so sumptuous, so sumptuous as to seem unreal... But I won't betray you. I won't tell anyone about that mad expense... about that lie to yourself that you bought with all your savings.

And I won't even sell this last one, the only real letter of the magnificent Gabriele, to make a little money. Though I could use it. You have willed to me a sublime swindle that has scalded my senses. Thank you, you are magnificent...
Addio Mamma, *addio* Gabriele!

Clarinet.

End

Mara entra in scena tenendo una scatola in braccio. Si siede su una poltroncina illuminata da una lampada a stelo. Apre la scatola e prende a leggere i fogli.

MARA

«Cara Barbara mia. Ieri ti scrissi breve. Non volevo dirti che la nevralgia mi tormentava molto. Mi pareva di non vederci più. La tua lettera mi consolò. Mangiai le violette che mi profumarono il cuore e mi parvero più dolci di qualunque frutto prezioso. Poi pensai a te a te, tutto tutto il giorno, con una indicibile tenerezza. Ricordai le più piccole vicende dei nostri amori, dal 2 aprile ad oggi per ordine, lentamente, provando talvolta un piacere singolare e talvolta una soffocazione di desiderio.

Addio. Ti bacio la bocca. Ti desidero molto. Dillo alla rosa originale» (17 marzo 1888).

Mara osserva il foglio in lungo e in largo.

Firmato: Gabriele... Gabriele... ma chi è?

Mara rigira fra le mani la lettera.

Cara Barbara... Mamma, questa lettera d'amore è indirizzata a te! Non mi hai mai detto che ricevevi lettere d'amore... ma quando l'hai conosciuto? dove? mamma, come? ...non riesco a crederci... Così, mentre passavi la scopa sui gradini brontolando, tu covavi un segreto così grande, così grande, mamma, non è possibile...

Mara riprende a leggere.

«Son quindici giorni che siamo lontani, un secolo intero, Barbara mia. Oggi è la mia festa. Ho la stanza piena di fiori. La giunchiglia, i narcisi e i giacinti odorano così forte ch'io mi sento un poco ubriaco. Però è una giornata grigia e pesante e irritante, forse come quella che ieri ti metteva nelle vene l'inquietudine. Oggi penserò a te molto. Mi sento assai languido. Se tu fossi qui passerei le ore fra le tue braccia a sognare e a farmi accarezzare come un gatto pigro e sonnacchioso. Quanto darei perché tu oggi facessi qui fra i fiori una apparizione! La tua bocca deve essere ardente come la fiamma e il tuo alito deve essere profumato come le rose che hai nel cuore. Addio Barbarella soave. Ti amo e ti chiamo, Gabriele».

Mara si ferma a riflettere. È sempre più sorpresa e stupita.

Come ti amava! Ma dove, dove lo nascondevi un amante così appassionato, che né io né papà ci siamo mai accorti di nulla! La maternità, la casa... io rido, io rido di chi pretende da una donna innamorata che essa si adegui, che prenda le sue ossa dolci e le chiuda dentro una tomba, ponendoci magari sopra una lapide: qui giace una madre che avrebbe potuto amare ma non lo fece per spirito di sacrificio! Tutto da ridere, tutto da ridere...

Mara riprende a leggere.

« Stamattina ti ho scritto mentre ero oppresso da una tristezza atroce. Per vincermi sono uscito e sono andato al mare. Su la rotonda di Castellammare ho veduto una bimba che aveva la tua bocca e li occhi tuoi e in certe movenze la tua espressione infantile.

Che strana somiglianza! Io non ho ancora veduto il tuo ritratto di quel tempo ma penso che dovevi essere così.

La bocca specialmente, oh la bocca! Quella bimba che ha quattro anni appena si chiama Elvezia. Le ho dato tanti baci su la faccia su li occhi, su i capelli. Ella mi guardava stupefatta e quasi sbigottita.

Sto molto male. Ho i nervi così scossi che a fatica mi riesce di scrivere. La mia mano trema e vacilla come quella di un paralitico.

Addio Barbarella buona. Ti bacio tutta. Senti ancora sul busto la mia ardente e dolcissima tunica di baci? Furono centosessanta. Ricordi? ti scrivo con l'anima profumata d'amore, di malinconia e di gelsomino mentre nella stanza accanto un amico suona il clarinetto... »

Si sente un suono di clarinetto. Mara bacia la lettera e guarda sognante il vuoto.

Una madre così piccola, insignificante. Una madre che non le avresti dato un soldo... Mamma, quelle tue ciabattine color uovo che infilavi sui piedi appena entravi in casa per non sporcare il pavimento. E li strusciavi per terra, come fossero lumache. Io ti guardavo camminare goffa e pensavo: povera, povera mamma che non ha avuto niente dalla vita. Ti vedevo giallina come quelle ciabattine. Avrei voluto baciarteli quei piedi minuscoli. Ma non osavo. Perché, piccola com'eri e paglierina, eri però severissima con me e non avresti gradito una confidenza. Mai. E invece tu nascondevi un tesoro incommensurabile!

Mara riprende a leggere.

«Ieri passai la giornata intera a preparare la mia stanza nel castello incantato. L'opera fu triste e pur dolce. Il tuo spirito era presente. Ogni cosa mi parlava di te. Se tu vedessi il "cuscino delle carezze" alla gran luce! I segni dell'amore ch'egli ha sostenuto sono evidenti... I fiori pallidi di seta sono diventati lucenti e un po' logori negli orli. E tutta la stoffa ha un odor singolare, sottilissimo ma percettibile alle mie narici esperte nell'aspirare le più tenue onde del profumo.

Ricordi i gridi alti della voluttà suprema? E i sonni che avevano una ineffabile soavità nella profonda stanchezza della carne? Ricordi tutto?

Ho teso alle pareti le tende e i tappeti. Ti aspetto. Ieri quando terminai di fare il tapezziere mi stesi sul divano col capo appoggiato al cuscino magico e sognai lungamente. Fra le tende verdi, sbattute dal vento, appariva il mare azzurro, popolato di vele rosse.

Sognai una vita men triste, una fatica men solitaria... Oh sentire la casa sonora gioir del tuo canto.»

Mara sorpresa.

Mamma, tu hai anche cantato! Io che non ho mai sentito la tua voce, se non nel rimprovero triste, severo. Storcevi la bocca con un piccolo movimento rabbioso e tetro. Tu cantavi!

Mara legge.

«Sentirmi d'improvviso cingere il collo e baciare la nuca... Riposarmi sul tuo corpo ignudo che ha la mollezza dei velluti più molli e il profumo d'un frutto sconosciuto!»

Mara commenta.

«La mollezza dei velluti», tu mamma che eri un
ferro. Perciò con quelle mani piccole, dure e dolenti
con cui tagliavi le cipolle, impastavi la farina, tra-
scinavi il ferro caldo sulle camicie di papà, con
quelle mani accarezzavi il corpo di un uomo che
moriva d'amore per te, di nascosto, dentro stanze
segrete, e poi tornavi a casa e riprendevi a pulire, a
cucire, a stirare... non è possibile.

Mara legge.

«Ieri, a punto, il desiderio di te mi prese con una
dolorosa veemenza. Era sul mezzogiorno. Io aveva
fatto il bagno nel mare e stava ignudo al sole su la
spiaggia. Era una deliziosa carezza dell'aria marina
mista all'odore dei raggi che mi avvolgevano tutto
in una rete d'oro.
    Chiusi gli occhi e mi persi nella contempla-
zione di te. D'un tratto la carezza fresca e mollis-
sima dell'aria sul mio corpo caldo mi diede
l'immagine viva del piacere d'un tempo. Sentii la
tua bocca, la tua bocca suggente, la voluttà mia
unica, la morte mia lenta e vicina, lo spasimo dolce
dell'anima mia» (14 luglio 1888).
    Che linguaggio suntuoso, che grazia serpentina!
una sensualità così morbida e lucida nello stesso
tempo! che uomo mamma! dove l'hai trovato un
uomo così appassionato e così bravo nel raccontare
la sua passione! E io dov'ero mamma quando tu lo
amavi? Perché non me l'hai fatto conoscere?

Riprendendo a leggere.

«Stamani al primo svegliarmi guardavo il mio
corpo arso dal sole. Da tutto il busto mi cadeva
l'epidermide, ma specialmente di su la spalla, nel

luogo dove tu posavi la testa. Con le dita strappavo
piano piano i brani della pelle e pensavo che forse
in quei brani morti era ancora il segno della tua
guancia e de' tuoi baci. Ho perduto la prima spoglia
come un serpente. Quanta voluttà quella spoglia ha
contenuto!

Sento la tua bocca su la mia gota e sul mio collo.
Si apre e si chiude mollemente strisciando, carez-
zevole e tentatrice. Quando mi baciavi così, allora
io ero perduto!»

Mara commenta.

Oh dio, dio grandissimo, come è possibile che tanto
uragano dei sensi sia passato per le nostre povere
stanze senza che noi ne fossimo consapevoli! Ora
capisco il senso di certe tue uscite, mamma. Dicevi
che andavi a cercare una stoffa da cucire. Dicevi
che andavi dalla sarta. E sparivi per due, tre ore.
Poi tornavi modesta, sempre chiusa nei tuoi ve-
stitini neri, accollati, con la faccia senza trucco, i
capelli tirati indietro sulla nuca. Chi poteva immaginare! ...Mamma, ti chiedo: ma chi eri? ...Chi
avevo io per madre? Una astuta simulatrice? Una
dolorosa e segreta innamorata del mistero? Una
cinica doppiogiochista? Una pazza incosciente?
Una bellissima fata dai capelli turchini? Io non so,
francamente non so più...

Clarinetto. Mara riprende a leggere.

«Ieri mattina rientrando nella mia stanza vidi
che il pastello col tuo ritratto non c'era più. Che
l'avesse portato via Carmelo di nascosto, forse per
ridere? Andai su al Convento, vidi Carmelo e gli
cominciai a dire delle parole amare, non so perché.
L'ira, a poco a poco m'invase, così che l'offesi

mortalmente senza riparo. Non ci vedevo più, non sapevo più quel che facevo e dicevo. Chi sa per quali ragioni fisiologiche io soggiacqui a quell'impeto feroce.

La follia mi durò qualche tempo. Rimasi tutto il giorno a letto con una febbre violenta. Ora sto meglio e ripenso con gran tristezza a questo strano fenomeno.

L'uomo forse è soggetto per necessità inevitabile a ritorni improvvisi e inesplicabili di bestialità primitiva?

Baciami la fronte, la faccia, la bocca, accarezzami, dimmi tante cose dolci e fraterne. Perdonami se non ti scrissi ieri, se ti scrivo così male oggi. Ti amo senza fine. E tu?»

Mamma, ti ricordi quando mi venivi a svegliare la mattina perché mi preparassi per la scuola? aprivi le finestre con un gesto brusco. Io gridavo: aspetta un momento mamma, la luce è troppo forte, mi acceca. Ma tu non mi davi retta. Facevi sbattere le due persiane contro le pareti esterne: pam, pam, e poi venivi verso il letto e con un gesto spartano tiravi via la coperta. Come ti odiavo!

Mara riprende a leggere.

«Questa notte è stata una notte terribile. Non ho mai chiuso li occhi, fra dolori atroci. Iersera sbagliai nel prendere una medicina: mandai giù una gran quantità di acido tartarico credendo di prendere un calmante. Ho riavuta la febbre. Ora sto meglio, ma ho i nervi così irritati e così deboli che tremo tutto al minimo rumore. I battiti del mio polso non hanno regola: a volte non si sentono, a volte sono così rapidi e forti che mi pare empiano del loro rumore tutta la stanza.

Desidero indicibilmente la tua compagnia. Non so che darei per averti qui, per leggerti nelli occhi per ritornare nella sicurezza del tuo amore. Com'è angoscioso il dubbio, quando lo spirito è così sottile e lucido per l'abuso de sogni che crede di vedere e di sentire.

Addio, amami e scrivimi. Il cielo è velato e il mare è grosso, metà color di fango e metà verdissimo. Io morirò di malinconia prima di sera, certamente, tuo Gabriele.»

Se tu avessi pronunciato questo nome: Gabriele, almeno una volta, mamma, almeno una volta. Il nome di un arcangelo furioso d'amore... Come facevi a conservarlo intatto e fermo nella bocca? Non ti veniva voglia di sputarlo fuori? Non ti saltava sulla lingua? non si insinuava fra le labbra come un serpentello impudico? Oh quel clarinetto che sguscia dalle oscure stanze della memoria epistolare!

Clarinetto. Mara riprende a leggere.

9 ottobre. «Stamani ho fatto una lunga passeggiata a cavallo. Che freddo improvviso! Nella notte la gran madre Majella s'era tutta coperta di neve; e la tramontana soffiava gelata e forte. Sono tornato al Convento dove sono ospite verso mezzogiorno. Guarda che cosa singolare! avevo meco il tuo ritratto barbarico.»

Fra sé.

Ritratto barbarico? Che sia quello che ti ho fatto io quando avevo tredici anni? Un occhio verde, uno nero, il naso color canarino, le labbra lilla, i capelli color mattone. Oh mamma, come ero fiera del mio dipinto! Senza volerlo avevo fatto un ritratto barbarico. Un ritratto barbarico!

Clarinetto. Mara legge.

«Tu nelle fotografie perdi assai, Barbara mia. L'immagine che ho di te nella mente "in cima dè pensieri miei" è più fulgida, più bella, più vivente, più amorosa, più desiderabile. Al ritratto barbarico, ti dirò, m'è sempre venuta la tentazione di tagliargli un occhio per metterlo dentro una breloque antica mandatami da mia madre. Resisto, resisto, ma finirò per tagliarti un occhio. Perdonami.

Io non ne posso più. M'intendi? Altro che i tuoi desideri e le tue malinconie. Io ho il furore. Di notte faccio sul letto certi salti e getto certe grida fra il sonno che è uno spavento per chi dorme nell'attigua stanza. I bagni freddi valgono. Mi guardo allo specchio: ho li occhi lucidi, quasi fiammeggianti, come uno che sia presso alla demenza, al delirio: occhi voraci. Ripenserai i baci, quelli che sai. Parliamo d'altro perché tremo come se avessi la terzana.

Nessuna carezza, ah, nessuna carezza varrà ad appagare il desiderio mio quando ti riavrò. Mi pare che, per esser pago io dovrei beverti divorarti metterti tutta dentro di me o entrar tutto dentro di te. Scegli!

Senti che tremo? Batto i denti come la prima volta quando sbigottisti in quella stanza misera e oscura. Addio addio addio. Mi pare di morire. Ti giuro Barbara mi par di morire, Gabriele.»

Fra sé.

Una donna sconosciuta nelle stanze di una casa troppo conosciuta. Un fantasma gentile, silenzioso, che pulisce, scopa, lava, stira e si porta dentro un gigantesco segreto che mai mai trapela agli occhi dei familiari. Mamma, sei un fenomeno! «Nessuna

carezza, nessuna carezza varrà ad appagare il
desiderio mio quando ti avrò». ...Come è ben
detto! «Il linguaggio», mamma, «rivela il corpo di
chi scrive». Così diceva il mio professore, Attanasio
Ghirelli e aveva ragione. Povero Ghirelli, con le sue
sciarpette unte, le sue dita gialle di nicotina, i suoi
baffetti grigi e gli occhi... gli occhi di cane triste,
perennemente lagrimosi e malinconici...

Mara Giannini, fu Gilberto Giannini, e fu...?
Fu, professore, no, è viva mia madre, e vive e
traffica come un topo, sempre di corsa, sempre di
corsa... scavando sottoterra cunicoli che io credevo
di passione familiare e invece no, erano di passione
erotica, di passione erotica, professor Giannini!

Mara riprende a leggere.

«Mia gelosia, i gelsomini mi hanno detto molte
tenerezze mentre i segni neri su la carta bianca mi
hanno detto cose che non comprendo ancora. Ho
serbato il profumo e non ho voluto pensare più
oltre al resto.

Ti scrivo di nuovo con l'anima profumata di
gelsomino, mentre ascolto distratto il suono del
clarinetto...»

Suono di clarinetto. Mara legge.

«Questa notte ho avuto la felicità di sognarti sempre. Su l'alba ti ho sognata così voluttuosamente
che sono venuto meno. Il mio letto è coperto di
quella coperta piccola in damasco rosso listata di
giallo ch'era a capo del nostro immenso e nascosto
talamo di una notte. Quanti strani spettacoli quel
damasco ha goduti! È pieno di suggestioni. I sogni
perfidamente dolci mi vengono forse da quel letto.

Non sopporto essere lontano da te. La sera ti

rimpiango, la notte ti rimpiango, la mattina ti rimpiango... ti rimpiango in tutte le ore, in tutti i minuti, in tutti gli attimi. Quando mi levo, alcune particolarità della mia toletta mi fanno trarre lunghi sospiri. Sorridi?

Mi portano in questo momento una tazza di caffè, una piccola tazza usuale. Oh quelle grandi tazze nerissime e fumiganti che tu mi versavi con un atto così gentile...Bevo un sorso e ti mando un bacio infinito. Anima, anima mia...»

Mara riflette.

Era geloso costui... Geloso, mamma, ma di chi? di me, vero? di me, certamente. Doveva sapere che le tue mani si posavano sul mio corpo, pazienti e gentili e non sul suo, come avrebbe voluto. Doveva sapere che ti chinavi su di me, la mattina e il tuo fiato dolce cadeva sulle mie palpebre ancora chiuse, doveva sapere di quelle tazze grandi di caffè bollente che preparavi per me e non per lui. Mio padre? Non credo proprio che potesse essere geloso di papà.

Sei proprio buffa mamma. Fai delle smorfie, anche da morta che proprio non si può fare a meno di ridere. Ma te lo ricordi come dormivate nello stesso letto, tu e papà, come se in mezzo a voi ci fossero i deserti del Sahara: uno raggomitolato sull'estremo confine dell'est e l'altro sull'estremo confine dell'ovest. Due continenti separati, due corpi che pur stando vicini non si incontrano mai. Mai.

Nemmeno una volta ho visto papà darti un bacio. Nemmeno quando ero piccola e tu eri giovane e fresca. Non l'ho mai visto prenderti una mano, o dirti una parola affettuosa. Entrava e usciva con quei suoi occhi scuri e malinconici, la faccia torva, la bocca serrata che ci sarebbe voluta una chiave speciale per aprirla e sembrava che in famiglia nessuno l'avesse mai posseduta.

Io poi mi chiedo perché vi siete sposati, mamma, perché? Ma sì lo so: eri incinta di me. Una volta me l'hai confessato, quasi senza volerlo. A mezza bocca, mamma, a occhi bassi... Mica c'è niente da vergognarsi. Lo so come succedono queste cose... "Siamo andati al cinema di nascosto perché tu sai, in paese non era ammesso che una ragazza e un ragazzo..." Mamma, tremavi mentre mi raccontavi di quella sera, sembravi presa dalla febbre... "Siamo andati al cinema di nascosto. E dopo il cinema, sul muretto della chiesa lui mi ha abbracciato forte e poi... poi mi sono trovata incinta e manco lo sapevo." Gloria in excelsis dei! quanto c'è voluto perché la tua confessione venisse fuori! Hai aspettato secoli. Solo quando ho compiuto ventun anni ti sei sentita in diritto, o forse in dovere, di raccontarmi questa storia del cinema e dell'abbraccio...

E quanti anni avevi, mamma, quando sei rimasta incinta? Diciannove? Quasi quanto me che ne avevo compiuti ventuno il mese prima e ancora ero vergine, vergine come una capra selvatica... non ci pensavo all'amore, avevo paura, una paura insensata, terribile. Ed eri tu, proprio tu mamma ad avermi inculcato quella paura. Tremavi, tremavo. Ti coprivi, mi coprivo. Scappavi, scappavo. Senza sapere niente, senza neanche immaginare che dietro quelle fughe c'era un altro amore, un altro desiderio, quello vero. Mamma, questa non me la dovevi fare! Mentre con me parlavi di compiti, di maestre, di scarpe, di cotolette, tu ascoltavi in cuor tuo il clarinetto di Gabriele! Maledetta maternità feroce!

Clarinetto. Mara legge.

«Quando penso che la causa prima dei tuoi dolori
e dei tuoi fastidii familiari sono io, mi punge un
rammarico indicibile e vorrei che tu conoscessi
tutta la mia passione per farmi perdonare il danno.
Sei tu certa che il mio amore valga il tuo dolore?
Ne sei certa, sicura, profondamente consapevole?
Tu non immaginerai giammai lo sbigottimento
ch'io ho nello spirito, La mia tortura maggiore è
questa implacabile lucidezza della visione fantas-
tica. Io ti vedo contorcerti nell'eccesso, io vedo i
tuoi lineamenti scomporsi e illividirsi, i tuoi occhi
volgersi disperatamente sotto le palpebre rosse di
pianto... Per quanti sforzi faccia non riesco a scac-
ciare l'orrida visione. E poi mi sento chiamare. Ho
proprio negli orecchi il suono della tua voce, un
suono roco e lamentevole come di chi chiede aiuto
e non ha speranze di aiuto...»

Mara commenta.

Ti ha fatto soffrire, mamma questo arcangelo
Gabriele, ti ha strizzata come uno straccio, ti ha
stretto la gola con le sue manine da seduttore.
Come hai potuto perdonarlo? Sapeva anche lui che
tu soffrivi, che avevi i lineamenti scomposti e
lividi... proprio così, proprio così... quante volte
tornando da scuola ti trovavo riversa sulla tavola
della cucina con la faccia contorta da una terribile
smorfia di sofferenza. Mamma, che hai? stai male?
no Mara, sto benissimo, vai a fare i compiti in
camera tua, vuoi che ti prepari un caffè? Sì mamma,
con tanto ghiaccio dentro. E volavo via coi libri,
col beverone di caffè e ghiaccio senza soffermarmi
sulla tua reticenza, sul tuo dolore, così a stento
trattenuto. Ma avresti parlato se ti avessi detto:

Parla? mi avresti raccontato di questo Gabriele che
ti torturava il corpo in segreto? Mamma, dimmi,
avresti parlato con la tua ranocchina, come mi
chiamavi qualche volta. La tua stupidissima ranoc-
chia che in tanti anni di convivenza non ha capito
niente di niente. Andavo a studiare Tacito. Come
una scema e mi sorbivo quel caffè, a piccoli sorsi,
anche quando era ormai ridotto solo ad acqua e
ghiaccio. Mamma, perché tradirmi così? io non ero
tuo marito, io potevo esserti amica. Perché non hai
mai detto una parola? E ora che sei morta mi butti
addosso questa valanga di parole d'amore e di
desiderio. Ma come si fa, come si fa?

Clarinetto. Mara legge.

«Io penso, penso, penso acutamente e l'acutezza del
pensiero mi dà uno spasimo inumano. Provo
talvolta una smania furibonda di strapparmi dalle
tempie dolenti questa cosa impalpabile che pure è
più forte e più inflessibile di un aculeo. Il respiro
m'è una fatica insopportabile e il battito delle vene
m'è fastidioso come il rimbombo di un martello
ch'io sia condannato ad ascoltare. È questo
l'amore? Oh no. Questa è una sorta di prodigiosa
infermità che fiorisce soltanto nel mio essere,
facendo la mia gioia e la mia pena.

...Io non avrò mai mai la pace interna e l'intera
sicurtà. Io non potrò mai esser pago se non a un sol
patto: assorbendo tutto tutto il tuo essere e di-
venendo con te un essere unico, vivendo della tua
vita, pensando i tuoi pensieri... Vorrei almeno che
i tuoi sensi fossero chiusi a qualunque sensazione
che non ti venisse da me...»

Mara commenta.

Che pretese! che possessività! come poteva pensare che lei mi cancellasse dalla sua vita? come poteva pretendere che non provasse niente, niente all'infuori del desiderio per lui! che arroganza, Gabriele mio, te lo devo dire, ha fatto bene mia madre a non accettare il tuo invito... Neghi di averla ossessionata con la domanda di lasciare tutto, marito figlia e casa per venire con te? Puoi negarlo? Ma lei, lei ha sempre rifiutato. È questo che ti dannava, dillo... non tolleravi la sua fedeltà alla famiglia, nonostante l'amore, nonostante il delirio dei sensi. La famiglia, caro Gabriele, è la sola realtà che conta, la sola ricordatelo... ma che dico? Io proprio io che l'ho odiata quella famiglia? ...la famiglia, la famiglia, quella cosa viscida e indecifrabile che sguscia, si sparge, sparisce per poi riapparire tutto d'un tratto come un drago assetato di carezze... Eppure, eppure, per quanto divisa, strappata, recisa, torturata, mia madre è rimasta fedele alla famiglia. Non c'è niente da fare. È così, è così....

Clarinetto. Mara legge.

«Ancora non comprendo, non comprendo la tua affezione per quell'uomo e non so difendermi da un sentimento iroso che va in parte anche contro di te. Per non tormentarti non ti scrivo in proposito i miei pensieri. Sono acerbi e oscurissimi. Sento che per qualche tempo la mia tenerezza è avvelenata. Credo che sia meglio che tu non mi riveda. Non tornare ora da me se vuoi evitare a te medesima un dolore inutile. Io non sono buono ora. L'anima mia ti ama e si prostra e il pensiero ti morde e ti macchia. E il contrasto ricomincia sempre, non finirà mai. Un dolore, un dolore atroce, ritorna...Voglio vederti, parlarti, carezzarti. Ti amo

come non mai... risparmiami però la vista delle tue
lividure. Io non so pensarci senza raccapriccio e
senza collera. Mi pare che se vedessi la tua carne
macchiata da quelle mani mi si spezzerebbe il
cuore...»

Mara riflette.

Forse tuo marito aveva capito. Per questo aveva
alzato le mani su di te, è così mamma? Un urlo nella
notte. Ancora mi si raggrinza la pelle. Io che ac-
corro e tu che dici: non è niente, niente Mara mia.
Ma ho visto la camicia stracciata e quei segni neri
sul collo. Aveva tentato di strangolarti, dillo, aveva
provato ad ucciderti, dillo! ...quell'uomo pacifico
e muto, quell'uomo grigio e metodico, aveva sco-
perto una lettera? Non lo saprò mai. Non lo saprò
mai.

   La portiera diceva che sulle uscite di mio padre
regolava l'orologio. Sette in punto, non un secondo
di più, non un secondo di meno: l'avvocato Gianni
Giannini, vestito di grigio perla, con i capelli grigio
argento, la borsa grigio topo, i baffetti grigio
piombo lustrati con un poco dell'olio di oliva
rubato in cucina – la sola stravaganza del suo
aspetto perfettamente anonimo – l'avvocato
Gianni Giannini usciva di casa a passo regolare,
entrava nella sua Polo grigio ferro, metteva in moto
e aspettava con ligia e grigia pazienza che il motore
si scaldasse. Mentre attendeva si accendeva una
sigaretta da cui sortiva un fumo grigio morbido e
riccioluto come una nuvola, e quando il motore si
era scaldato, schiacciava l'acceleratore, tenendo le
braccia tese sul volante, per andare a vivere la sua
giornata tutta regolata da norme grigie come l'a-
sfalto bagnato.

È proprio strano che abbia capito qualcosa dei segreti della mamma. La sua vita non era preparata per sorprese di nessun genere. I fatti imprevedibili erano esclusi dalle sue giornate, tutte accuratamente preparate in precedenza, senza alcuna possibilità di una irruenza dell'imprevisto.

Solo con me qualche volta si permetteva una trasgressione: vuoi un gelato Marina? Era il solo a chiamarmi Marina. «La mia Marina profumata», diceva e mi prendeva per mano. Papà, andiamo al cinema? papà, andiamo a pattinare? Sì bambina, domenica. Io ci voglio andare oggi. Vacci con la mamma. Ma la mamma aveva troppo da fare. Papà, ti prego... la sua bocca si piegava in un sorriso amaro e rimproverante. Lui non approvava il tuo modo di educarmi, così spartano e severo, mamma, lui non approvava niente di niente.

E Gabriele sarebbe stato geloso di un uomo così? Geloso di quel letto, di quel corpo? Un marito è un marito, bambina mia... come sottrarsi? Ti scappava da ridere. Ti mettevi una mano davanti alla bocca. Perché così eri stata abituata. Come una vera contadina.

Clarinetto. Mara legge.

«Qui tutto è violenza, spasimo, eccesso. Dove sono le mie delicatezze? Dove sono le mie malinconie squisite e complicate? dove sono le afflizioni profonde e tortuose in cui l'anima si perdeva come in labirinti inestricabili?

Tu partivi, tu partivi senza ch'io ti potessi vedere, e coprirti di baci la faccia! Verso le undici come per istinto mi voltai. Entrava tuo marito con due amici. Mi prese una convulsione di dolore così forte che dovetti alzarmi poco dopo e uscire.

Ma io dubito. Ho contro di te oggi l'animo
ostile. Sono pieno di un'ira compressa. Uscirò tra
poco e andrò in mare. Le onde sono allegre e forti.
Addio. Non ti scrivo più per non dirti cose durissime. Addio. Mi ami tu? O scrivi ancora d'amore
per abitudine pietosa? Sei tu leale? che pensi? che
fai? Io soffro. Ho il diritto di interrogarti così.
Dubito, dubito, dubito. Sono demente...»

Mara riflette.

Io giuro che mia madre era leale, lealissima... come
puoi dubitare della sua buona fede? Come puoi
pensare di dire «cose durissime» ad una donna che
soffre, che si torce, si lacera nel dolore di doversi
dividere fra...

Ma ne sei proprio sicura Mara? sei proprio
sicura che tua madre fosse leale? verso chi? ma se
ti ha mentito sempre? se ha mentito a suo marito
per anni! ha mentito a te, innocente, con una
astuzia da volpe segreta e notturna, potrebbe avere
mentito anche a lui, all'amante.

Clarinetto. Mara legge.

«Dove sei? oltre quali terre? oltre quali mari? Passo
le ore nell'inerzia pensando. Questa mia stanza è
diventata funebre come una cappella sotterranea.
Talvolta io mi vedo disteso in una bara; io mi
contemplo nella immobilità della morte, con una
lucidezza imperturbabile...»

Mara legge.

«Le rondini garriscono passando e ripassando a
stormi come nere saette, nel rettangolo pallido
segnato dal balcone. Che cosa mi manca? qual è il
difetto del mio organismo morale? qual è la causa

della mia impotenza? Io ho una brama ardentissima di vivere, di svolgere in ritmo tutte le mie forze di sentirmi completo e armonioso. E ogni giorno invece io perisco segretamente, ogni giorno la vita mi sfugge da varchi invisibili e innumerabili. Tutte le mie forze non ad altro mi servono che a trascinare con una immensa fatica qualche granello di polvere a cui la mia immaginazione dà il peso d'un macigno gigantesco».

Mara riflette.

Ma da dove viene tutto questo scontento? Non era lo scontento di lei ma di sé... che inquietudine! che insoddisfazione irrimediabile! Ma perché? Eppure quella insoddisfazione io la conosco... mi pare una cosa mia... Quante volte mi faccio le stesse domande? ...E se io fossi ...se io fossi figlia di quell'uomo? Nascere dall'amore, per quanto segreto, dissestato, clandestino, infelice, sarà più propizio che nascere dall'abitudine quotidiana e dall'indifferenza!

Clarinetto. Mara legge.

«C'è sulla terra una sola ebbrezza durevole: la sicurtà del possesso di un'altra creatura, la sicurtà assoluta, incrollabile. Io cerco questa ebbrezza. Io vorrei poter dire: la mia amante, vicina o lontana, non vive se non del pensiero di me. Ella è sottomessa con gioia ad ogni mio desiderio, ha la mia volontà per unica legge. S'io cessassi d'amarla, ella morirebbe.

È un'ora molle, discreta, propizia alle sensualità delicate. Oh se tu fossi qui con me! ...Dormirò ancora una volta solo. Se tu vedessi il letto! È un letto rustico, un monumento, altare d'Imeneo, largo quanto un'aia, profondo come il sonno del giusto. È il Talamo dei Talami. Le materasse contengono la lana di un intero gregge e il pagliericcio contiene le foglie di un intero campo di granoturco».

Fra sé.

«Un'ora molle, discreta, propizia alle sensualità delicate...» Quest'uomo, che io già ho eletto a padre, mi fa vedere le cose, come fossero davanti ai miei occhi. Scolpisce le parole e per quanto siano di pietra le fa diventare aeree e preziose... dolcissime. Decisamente, mamma, io spero che tu mi abbia concepita in quel letto, fra quelle materasse che contenevano la lana di un intero gregge...

Clarinetto. Mara continua a leggere.

« Io so che l'amore è la più grande fra le tristezze umane perché è il supremo sforzo che l'uomo tenta per uscire dalla solitudine del suo essere interno: sforzo come tutti gli altri inutile. Ma pure io tendo all'amore con invincibile trasporto. So bene che l'amore, essendo un fenomeno, è la figura passeggera, ciò che si trasforma perennemente. Ma è proprio quello a cui aspiro, alla perpetuità dell'amore, a un amore che riempia una intera esistenza. Anche se so che la fragilità della donna è incurabile. Ma io non posso rinunciare alla speranza che la mia donna sia costante e fedele fino alla morte».

Mara commenta.

Si conosce, si analizza... e con che acutezza! ...Gabriele, Gabriele mio, se pur da lontano, se pur ignorando come sei fatto, se pur attraverso la mia piccola sciagurata madre materna, io oggi potrei innamorarmi di te... Ma un ritratto suo, un ritratto dell'arcangelo, mamma, possibile che tu non l'abbia conservato?

Frugando nella scatola.

Nessuna fotografia, nessun disegno, niente.

Clarinetto. Mara legge.

«Con queste attitudini, io rimango disutile e o-zioso... Avendo preso a dubitare di me, a poco a poco sono giunto a dubitare di tutto. Avendo cominciato a soffrire di me, a poco a poco ho cominciato a soffrire in tutto. Mi sento schiacciare dalla universale stupidezza... Talvolta un pensiero mi occupa, unico, assiduo: il pensiero della morte. In quei momenti ogni impressione passa sul mio spirito come una goccia d'acqua su una lastra rovente: o rimbalzando o dissolvendosi. Io ho pietà di me, capisci, e conosco la voluttà della compassione: una misteriosa tristezza in cui mi indugio.

Ecco, forse ora mi conosci meglio e sai con chi hai a che fare, Barbara mia. Io sono quell'uomo dall'invincibile libidine ereditaria, che pure si compiace, nella delicatezza più fragrante di chiamare sorella la sua amata, avido di comunioni spirituali».

Clarinetto. Mara legge.

«Eppure questa donna è stata di altri prima che mia, mi dico, ti dico. Essa ha giaciuto con un altro uomo, ha dormito con un altro uomo nel medesimo letto, sul medesimo guanciale... Questo mi ripeto. In tutte le donne è singolarmente viva una specie di memoria fisica, la memoria delle sensazioni. Ti ricordi delle sensazioni avute da colui? Non puoi non ricordare... Puoi avere dimenticato l'uomo che ti violò? Cosa provavi sotto le carezze del marito?»

Mara commenta.

Carezze del marito? solo una fantasia esaltata poteva andare a scovare un gesto lì dove non c'era che vuoto... Ma come accontentare un tale desiderio di possesso? Niente al mondo l'avrebbe saziato, niente al mondo...

Clarinetto. Mara legge.

«Io avrei voluto che tu mi dicessi: Ecco, mi prendi vergine. Io non conosco nessuna voluttà dell'amore. Questo avrei voluto sentire dalle tue labbra. Anche se io so che tu ti sei trasformata a imitazione mia, avendo preso i miei pensieri, i miei giudizi, i miei gusti, i miei dispregi, le mie predilezioni, le mie malinconie, tutto ciò che dà ad uno spirito una speciale impronta, un carattere... Ma prima, amore caro, prima che ci incontrassimo, tra quali umilianti contatti hai trascorso le ore lontane? È questo che mi ossessiona, è questo che non tollero. Ripenso alle volte che ti ho visto allontanarti per tornare alla casa del marito, nella casa di un uomo a me interamente ignoto, nella volgarità e nella meschinità della vita borghese, in mezzo alle quali sei nata e sei cresciuta come una pianta rara in mezzo alle ortaglie. Non mi hai mai nascosto nulla? Non mi hai mai ingannato? Hai sempre potuto sottrarti al desiderio di tuo marito, col pretesto della malattia? Sempre? puoi giurarlo?»

Mara commenta.

Sempre, posso giurarlo!

Clarinetto. Mara legge.

«Guardandoti dormire, creatura delicata e complicata, chiusa nel mistero del sonno, parevi raggiare da tutti i pori una fascinazione occulta, d'una incredibile intensità... e io ho avvertito in fondo a me ancora una volta un vago moto di istintivo terrore.

Io non posso riflettere, non posso reprimere questa folle insurrezione di paure, di sospetti, di dubbi... Avrei voglia di gridarti: non t'amo più, tutto è finito, la fiamma è spenta.»

Mara legge.

«Tu diventi ogni giorno più puerile negli atti, nei gusti, nei desideri. Fra me e te non corrono se non reazioni di sensualità raffinata. Tu porti anche nei piaceri amorosi quello studio e quella lentezza con cui assapori i frutti che prediligi, con cui prolunghi qualunque altra piccola delizia, mostrando di non volere vivere per altra cosa, ponendo ogni tua cura nel coltivare e nell'ornare le tue e le mie sensazioni. Le tue pause di silenzio e di immobilità non provengono se non da stanchezza muscolare...»

Clarinetto. Mara legge.

«Distruggere per possedere. Non ha altri poteri chi cerca nell'amore l'Assoluto... Se io possedessi la vera fede, quella fede che permetteva a Santa Teresa di vedere Iddio realmente nell'ostia! Dove, dove trovare il segreto della mia infelicità e della mia debolezza!

Chi ucciderà il desiderio? amore mio! Ho visto nell'alba sacra dei tempi, in un giardino delizioso, il primo uomo solitario e triste che attirava la prima compagna. E questa diveniva in breve tempo il flagello del mondo, spargendo ovunque dolore e morte. Ma la voluttà come peccato mi appare più fiera, più agitante. Nessun'altra ebbrezza come quella frenetica degli amplessi mi pare simile a quella a cui si abbandonavano i martiri della Chiesa primitiva nelle prigioni, aspettando il supplizio.»

Clarinetto. Mara legge.

«Ti sembro crudele anima mia? Ma pure io vedo che c'è un aspetto distruttivo in te, più palese quanto più forte è il tuo orgasmo nelle carezze... Nel buio della notte sorge l'immagine terrifica e quasi gorgonea della donna quale mi sei apparsa più volte, fra le palpebre socchiuse, a me convulsa in uno spasimo o inerte in uno sfinimento e-stremo... Come quella volta che ti togliesti lo spillo che fermava il garofano nei capelli e te lo ponesti fra le labbra. Poi pianamente apristi il pugno, pren-desti la farfalla prigioniera per le ali e ti accingesti a trafiggerla. Che crudeltà, ti dissi, come sei crudele! Ma tu sorridesti, intenta all'opera, mentre la piccola vittima batteva le ali già sfiorite. Ti brillavano gli occhi! ...Tu sei una donna taciturna e triste che cova dentro di sè il male sacro, il morbo astrale; tu sei l'amante cupida e convulsa il cui ardore è talvolta quasi spaventevole, la cui lussuria ha talvolta apparenze quasi lugubri d'agonia...»

Mara pensa.

Morbo astrale... amante cupida e convulsa... ma perché, perché questo rivoltarsi di un corpo in-namorato. Cosa era successo? perché?

Mara legge.

«L'uomo fiacco, oppresso, titubante, infermiccio che sono ha prestato l'orecchie ad un grande filosofo poeta. Ho ascoltato la voce nuova che schernisce con aspri sarcasmi la debilità, l'irritabilità, la sensibilità morbosa, il culto della pietà, il vangelo della rinuncia, il bisogno di credere, il bisogno di umiliarsi, il bisogno di redimersi, tutti insomma i più ambigui bisogni spirituali dell'epoca, tutta la ridevole e miserevole effeminazione della vecchia anima europea, tutte le mostruose rifioriture della lue cristiana nelle razze decrepite.

L'uomo solitario, il contemplatore, lo speculatore inerte che sono io, ha teso l'orecchio con una strana ansietà a quella voce che afferma la vita, che considera il dolore come la disciplina dei forti, che ripudia ogni fede e in specie la fede nella Morale, che proclama la giustizia della ineguaglianza, che esalta le energie terribili, il sentimento della potenza, l'istinto di lotta e di predominio, l'eccesso delle forze generatrici e fecondanti, tutte le virtù dell'uomo dionisiaco, del vincitore, del distruttore, del creatore».

Mara pensa.

Ha smesso di parlare d'amore. Il suo discorrere è diventato amaro, sprezzante... Era dolce quando chiedeva baci, certezze. Ora invece le sue lettere sono diventate cupe, feroci. Dove è finito tutto quell'ardore?

Mara legge.

«Io non posso che aspirare ad una fine. E per mettere fine a tutti i sogni io non devo se non sognare di non volere più sognare. Non è forse il donare un bisogno? il ricevere non equivale forse all'avere pietà?

Tra me e l'altra, mia cara Anima, non c'è che una pura amicizia. Io avrei voluto che tu avessi letto

anche le altre lettere per convincerti della mia
innocenza. In quel piccolo biglietto tu hai letto
male una parola. Non devi parlare di "partage",
non c'è nessun partage. Ella non è che un'amica e
ti dirò anche di qual genere. E sapeva di te io le
parlavo di te. Il suo dono del pugnale fu fatto per
Natale e io scrissi sull'erba la data. Ma siccome ti
conoscevo straordinariamente sospettosa, tentai di
impedirti che tu leggessi. Ti prego, comprendimi.
Voglio che tu sia sempre la buona, la nobile amante,
l'amante sublime che ha saputo perdonare un'altra
volta, pur essendo certa della mia colpa. Tu sai
quanto ti amo e che ti preferisco a qualsiasi altra
creatura in terra. Tu sei l'unica, ora e sempre»
(lettera del 14 aprile 1892).

Mara pensa.

Come hai potuto sopportare tutto questo tor-
mento? questa tempesta di parole bugiarde? ...Tu
ti nascondevi, nascondevi, ritirandoti come una
lumaca nel suo guscio, il tuo dolore. E io che non
ho mai sospettato niente!

Clarinetto. Mara legge.

«Come mi fa male la tua piccola lettera! Quando io
sono sconfortato, m'inchino verso di te, con una
trepidazione profonda, sperando di udire la buona
parola consolatrice, perché ti conosco forte e
dritta, pietosa e consapevole. Perdonami se non ho
saputo intenderti, perdonami se non ho saputo
alleggerirti una pena, perdonami se non ho saputo
essere per te il fratello buono e coraggioso che tu
meritavi. Ma come mi fa male la tua piccola lettera
di addio. Dopo quattro anni d'amore e di intimità,
io apro ancora una tua lettera con le dita tremanti

e mi sento un nodo alla gola. Perdonami, perdonami i dubbi e le offensive certezze. Non sono io che dubito: è qualcuno in me, un essere malsano e malvagio che mi ubriaca di vapori torbidi e mi toglie la ragione. Addio addio. Prega per me.Pensami ed amami. Ti bacio la bocca: tuo Gabriele» (lettera del 14 giugno 1892).

Mara commenta.

Come reggere allo strazio di una separazione che tu hai voluto... perché è così, vero, è così? sei tu che l'hai voluta, sei tu che hai spedito la lettera di addio. Ma io ti capisco, ti capisco con tutto il cuore, ti capisco mamma, so che avevi ragione di allontanarti prima che fosse lui ad abbandonarti con impazienza. Il tuo orgoglio ti ha salvata. Ma è giusto dire che ti ha salvata? Le lettere sono finite. La tua storia si è conclusa rapidamente. Quattro anni di gloria che ti sei portata nella tomba con elegante cocciutaggine, con feroce gelosia... Se tu ne avessi parlato con me... non credi che ti avrei capita? Mamma, rispondi, non credi che ti avrei capita?

Ma qui c'è un altro foglio. Un foglio dentro una busta...

Prende la lettera, la osserva.

Un'altra lettera di rammarico? una lettera di scuse? ma a che serve ormai? la pena è consumata.

Apre la lettera. Legge.

«Cara Barbara, la vostra lettera profumata mi ha conquistato. Vi avevo risposto di no, che non si possono vendere le proprie memorie, o per lo meno non si possono vendere a chi è animato da pulsioni feticistiche, come mi sembra che siano le vostre. Ma poi, rileggendo la vostra delicata e dolorosa missiva ho ripensato alla proposta e sono arrivato a più miti consigli. Cosa c'è di male ad acconsentire ad un piccolo contratto privato fra due persone adulte che hanno una comune propensione per i sogni e le parole d'amore? Mi scuso per quel primo no che certamente vi avrà ferita. Ma ora sono qui da voi, col cappello in mano e la faccia contrita. Non so se sia stato il profumo della vostra lettera che è penetrato con sottile persistenza nelle mie narici, o se sono state le vostre parole gentili, umili, e nello stesso tempo appassionate che mi hanno fatto cambiare idea. Ma lo sapete che avete qualcosa dell'altra Barbara, oltre al nome? Lo sapete che la vostra devota persistenza mi ha ricordato un'altra devota persistenza a me tanto cara e familiare?

Sono pronto a scommettere che anche voi siete dotata di mani leggere e nervose... sono pronto a scommettere che anche i vostri capelli sono gonfi e morbidi e invitano le labbra a posarvisi sopra... Indovino? Quasi quasi vi supplicherei di incontrarmi. Sono un visitatore segreto e discreto... Ma non voglio turbarvi... so che avete un marito e una figlia... Vi lascio intera e integra a questi sacri affetti...

Piuttosto, mi avete offerto cinquecento lire per avere le mie lettere a Barbara che ella stessa mi restituì nel momento del commiato... Come vi ho detto, acconsento, purchè queste lettere rimangano a casa vostra, purchè non vengano pubblicate, purchè colei a cui erano dirette non giunga a sapere che ve le ho cedute... Il fatto è che mi trovo in un frangente difficile in cui anche quei pochi soldi possono decidere del mio futuro.

Vi propongo mille lire e le lettere saranno vostre. Acconsentite? Se mi spedirete un vaglia telegrafico, vi invierò subito le lettere. Certamente saprete che in pochi anni varranno il triplo. E voi potrete rivenderle facilmente. Vi saluto cara Barbarina... quel nome, voi lo sapete, mi è caro, gravido di ricordi suntuosi e tenerissimi... quel nome fantasma, ombra di un lontano potentissimo amore... quel nome mi risuscita nella memoria gesti innocenti e fascinosi... sento in voi la ripetizione di una sacrale offerta votiva: voi, simulacro della lontana e perduta Barbara amorosa, mi offrite il petto profumato di adultera perché vi appoggi ancora una volta il capo stanco e troppo innamorato...

Scrivetemi ancora caro fantasma profumato. Le vostre parole affettuose sono ambrosia per me... E non dimenticate il telegramma. L'indirizzo è: Gabriele D'Annunzio, presso Michetti, Lungomare Garibaldi, Francavilla, Abruzzo. Il suo Gabriele D'Annunzio.»

Mara lascia cadere la lettera. Esterrefatta. Pausa di sorpresa.

Con mille lire, mamma, con mille lire mi hai ingannata, turlupinata, sedotta, circuita, rallegrata, immalinconita, illusa, divertita, addolorata frodata, abbindolata, amareggiata, tradita, delusa, raggirata, irretita... con mille lire, mi hai fatto patire e gioire. Con mille lire... solo con mille lire... che... che allora però, lo so, lo so hai ragione all'epoca della tua giovinezza, erano tante, tantissime...

Canterellando.

...se potessi avere mille lire al mese... Chissà

quanto hai patito per metterle da parte, lira su lira... mollichella su mollichella... Ma come avrai fatto che non disponevi di un soldo, povera formicuzza mia... I sogni però si pagano e tu, da brava massaia, ti sei pagata coi risparmi, magari facendo la cresta sul pane, rubando sui soldi della spesa, povera madre mia, ti sei pagata il tuo sogno privato, il tuo sogno segreto, talmente suntuoso, talmente suntuoso da apparire irreale... Ma io non ti tradirò. Non dirò a nessuno di quella folle spesa... di quella menzogna a te stessa che hai pagato con tutti i tuoi risparmi.

E neanche venderò quest'ultima, la sola vera lettera del magnifico Gabriele. Per fare un pò di soldi. Eppure ne avrei bisogno. Mi hai lasciato in eredità una sublime turlupinatura che mi ha scaldato i sensi. Grazie, sei magnifica... Addio mamma, addio Gabriele!

Clarinetto.

Fine

Branko Gorjup: I'd like to start our conversation by asking a question about "judicial" violence and abuse of power. Some of our readers may not be aware that as a child you lived for two years with your parents during WW II in a Japanese internment camp. What were your parents doing at that time in Japan and why were they interned?

Dacia Maraini: My father went to Japan on a scholarship to study the people of Haynu. As he had just graduated in ethnology, this was a great opportunity for him. He had also recently married my mother, whose family was of the old but impoverished Sicilian aristocracy. The two had fallen in love and married against the wishes of their respective families – her family disapproved of the fact that he was not noble and his blamed her for not being rich. They moved to Florence, ate boiled potatoes and suffered the cold because of lack of money. But their love for each other was great and they were happy – the photographs from those years show my mother as a beautiful young woman with bright eyes. She used to paint and loved the outdoors, joining my father on his frequent mountain climbing, swimming, and skiing adventures. I consider myself as having had good fortune to be born to parents full of the joy of life, full of exciting projects, who surrounded me with much love and affection. I believe these are some of the reasons why I turned out to be fundamentally a positive and optimistic person.

When I was one year old, my parents left for Japan with a few pieces of luggage and a great deal of hope. They felt strong because of their reciprocal love, not afraid to face an uncertain future in an unknown country. When we arrived, we settled in Sapporo, known as the village of the snow. For six months a year our house would be buried and often the only way to get out was through the windows. I remember going to nursery school on a sleigh drawn by my mother. At this time, the war hardly touched us. The Japanese people were tolerant of foreigners. Our neighbors showed a great deal of love and trust towards us.

In 1943 things suddenly changed. The Japanese government demanded that the Italians living in Japan sign affiliation to the Republic of Salò, which by then had become the last Nazi/Fascist outpost in Italy. As my parents were anti-fascists – not so much for ideological as for moral and cultural reasons – they refused to comply. My father hated racism. He used to tell me, a four-year-old child: "Remember, there are no races, only cultures. Races do not exist." My mother, in her own right, loathed the vulgarity of the Fascists, finding them arrogant and brutal. So they decided not to associate themselves with the Republic of Salò. The following day, the police arrived and declared us officially "traitors," locking us up in a house under strict surveillance. We were not allowed to leave the house for any reason and a few days later a truck came by to pick us up. By this point we were a family of five as two of my younger sisters, Yuki and Tony, had been born in Japan in the early 1940s. We travelled south to Nagoya, to an internment camp.

B.G.: How vivid are your memories of those years?

D.M.: They are very clear, which is usually true of people who suffered a great deal. Physical and psychological pain engraves itself in one's mind as if branded with fire.

B.G.: In your fictionalized autobiography, which covers the early years in Bagheria, Sicily, following your family's return from Japan in 1947, you make only a few passing remarks on the time spent in the internment camp. Why? Is it because young Dacia, by being naturally overwhelmed with her new Italian experience, was able to push aside that painful past, or because mature Dacia, the writer, was not comfortable in confronting those memories? In, *Beloved Writing,* your most recent book of non-fiction, you confess that you haven't yet found "the right relationship" with this material. Why is it so difficult for the victims of oppression to make their stories public? How would you describe the *right* relationship with the material, which, as you say, "demands to be committed to writing?"

D.M.: It's true that I have been trying for years to write about my experiences in the internment

camp, without ever succeeding. There is some
sort of resistence coming from inside me. As
soon as I try, my thoughts and words are
blocked – it's as if I couldn't find the right
language for the kind of fear and suffering
experienced in those two years.

B.G.: All your work – novels, plays, stories, poetry,
including journalism – deals with a sense of
enclosure, imprisonment, and jail-break, not
always successful. Whether physical or mental,
political or cultural, this closing-in of individu-
als, putting them against their will or their
better knowledge into political lagers, reserves,
institutions or stereotypes, has been for centuries the cause of much suffering. To what extent can this concern of yours be ascribed to
your childhood experience in Japan and to
what extent to your subsequent education?

D.M.: It's possible that the experience of the internment camp influenced my vision of the
world in a way that has become inclusive. I
don't know. After I left the internment camp,
I stayed silent, speechless as it were, for a few
years. But the reason for this could have also
been that I changed countries and languages. I
spoke fluent Japanese, or rather the dialect of
Kyoto, the city we were staying in before they
transported us to the camp. So when we re-
turend to Italy, I was not able to express myself.
I was afraid of everything, even of crossing the
street or entering a shop. I was paralyzed by an
extreme form of shyness. At night I kept
dreaming about the war, the bombs, hunger

and the threats of guards. This is the reason why I started to write – it was easier for me to express myself in writing than orally. I would be terrified to face a person in front of me. While in a boarding school in Florence, I used to write, even to the Madonna, because I was unable to communicate orally my continuous obsessions with death. Still today, when I have something important to say to a person, I prefer to do it in writing. Writing, unlike spoken language, gives me greater freedom.

B.G.: Would you consider yourself a political writer? One who aims at improving the world by revisiting in fiction the sites that are extraneous to immediate experience, removed in time, and of concern to society as a whole? Or is this a misreading? Can political writing be also personal and private?

D.M.: I don't consider myself a political writer, except perhaps indirectly. It is true that I've always been appalled by injustice. But there is a big difference between indignation and political statement. When I write a novel, I try to listen to the characters who come and visit me and tell me their stories. When I write for newspapers, instead, I take sides, declare my indignation, clarify my reasons.

Fiction is more complex, deeper. Politics, on the other hand, has a lot more to do with the rules of behavior in society: up to what point can the individual freedom damage the freedom of the people as a collective? Up to what point can individual pleasure be limited

by social responsibility? And so on. And, as I
mentioned before, there are the characters who
are knocking at my door, asking to be narrated.
In this sense I'm a follower of Pirandello. Though
I project upon them something that is mine, they
possess nevertheless lives of their own. They are
not mere puppets, as some may think, who fall
lifeless when we stop moving them. Characters
are more like children, born from our own bodies, made of blood and flesh, with their own
identity, walking the earth on their own legs.
They are unforeseeable and mysterious and we
must be humble enough to listen to their voices.
This has nothing to do with politics but rather
with the complexity of being human, of living in
a world where there is more shadow than light,
more uncertainty then certainty.

B.G.: Feminism – in its wide variety of manifestations
– is certainly an aspect of your writing. It has
drawn a great deal of attention, from both the
critics and the general public, making your name
known throughout Italy and beyond. How and
when did you become conscious of yourself as a
female writer, writing decidedly from the point
of view of a woman about women's issues? Who
were your models? Were there any feminist
movements in Italy at that time?

D.M.: My feminism, if we wish to call it that, goes
back to my childhood. As a little girl, I came to
realize that girls were treated differently from
boys, that there existed a creepy sort of racism
directed against women, which expressed itself
in words, gestures, thoughts, ideologies and

repressive and misogynous religious rituals. Certainly, my infantile feminism manifested itself in blind indignation and instinctive revolt – at the time, I would not have been able to speak in theoretical terms. In 1969 I met for the first time a feminist group called Feminine Revolt. I joined the group and helped it find its headquarters. I was present at their group meetings but soon discovered I was not convinced. The reason was the group's authoritarianism and mysticism. As I've always hated intolerance of any kind, I left the group and attached myself to another called Pompeo Magno – named after the street where it used to meet – which was much more democratic. From this association, I learned many things about myself as a woman from the experiences of other women in the group. I learned how to look at history from the point of view of women and how to recognize with greater precision the injustices committed against them, without getting entangled in my personal story. And I learned how to distance myself when arguing, analyzing and interpreting facts. But what really interested me was producing art. As I've already said, I'm not a politician. Thus, I gathered women who shared my ideas and founded a theatre, La Maddalena, which gave space to women, not only as actresses or costume designers – the only roles occupied by them in the traditional theatre – but also as playwrights, directors, musicians and so on. We even created a school for women electricians, some of whom later went on to work in other theatres.

B.G.: We've come to understand, and, I guess, appreciate the fact, that there isn't only one kind of feminism. Women from different cultures have lived under different kinds of patriarchal dominance, which has meant choosing different paths to freedom. What have the Italian women, including yourself, found particularly difficult to fight in the Italian patriarchal system?

D.M.: The Church. The Church has entered our culture in an inextricable way, has become part of our experience, both positive and negative. For example, the image of the Madonna, beautiful, humble, obedient and dumb has been a model for many centuries, a model that has been imposed as the only possible one for a woman getting ready for marriage and maternity. The Madonna, as a model, is an oppressive image but also an image of enchantment and seduction. How many Madonnas, gentle, loving, seductive, with naked breasts, entered our infantile memory through the iconography of the great painting of the past? How do we get away from such a model without betraying our own history?

The Church has established a series of rules based on "decency," which have bitterly conditioned the lives of our grandmothers and great-grandmothers. The Church has declared the impurity of the female body and its sexuality dangerous. The consequence was to control, to dominate every impulse of the female soul. How do we get out of this?

Having said this, I believe that patriarchism

is more or less the same all around the world. The priority of every power, secular or religious, has always been to impose control over the female body and its reproductive capability, to be later followed by moral and psychological restrictions. At its root, patriarchism disesteems women. It is far easier for women to remedy legal and social wrongs than to create a profound esteem and trust toward themselves and other women. The lack of self-esteem often turns women into their own worst enemy.

B.G.: How successful has the Italian movement been? I'm still mesmerized watching the Italian Parliament in session, seeing mostly men. Why are there so few women entering politics in Italy?

D.M.: Feminism in Italy has touched all social classes – it has been a great revolution of the 20th century. Yet the situation in which it found itself as a movement was difficult and backward. So once the initial exaltation was over, the old ways of dividing sexual roles re-surfaced again, proving how difficult it is to change social habits. It should be enough that I quote a recent address made by the Pope to the world of the faithful, using the following metaphor: "The Church for Italy is a spouse and a mother, yet there is another female trying to insinuate herself into this sacred relationship. This woman, a prostitute, driven by sex and power, is bound to destroy the family union." Is this a forward-looking way of reasoning? Under many aspects, our Pope is certainly a courageous and advanced man, but he is definitely backward when it comes to defining sexual roles. And don't forget, today he is one of the most listened-to authorities in Italian society.

B.G.: With regards to the male-female relationship, what appears to emerge in your writing is a notion that the differences that separate men and women are not defined by biology, but rather by education. If this is so, these differences can eventually also be eradicated through education. Some feminist writers emphasize biological determinism, according to which the differences are an essential factor in the creation of a distinctively female literature, language, a way of being in the world. How have you come to your own position?

D.M.: It is true, as you noted, that the differences are always cultural. Biology is an excuse to impose a vision of the world that offends the rights of those who are weaker. Every form of racism is based on "natural" differences. I don't want to imply that women and men are identical. There are biological differences but the mentality, the roles that follow are the result of the power that one sex exerts over the other. Margaret Mead, the great American anthropologist, from whom I learnt a great deal, has shown with her studies that the concept of maternity, virginity, adultery, fatherhood and so on, changes according to the need of a people in regulating the production of children in relation to the exigencies of war and famine.

B.G.: You were a co-founder of a feminist theatrical co-operative, called La Maddalena. This was early on in your writing career, which coincided with your growing interest in the theatre. Why did the group organize and what was its aim? You were deeply involved over a long period of time, weren't you?

D.M.: The Theatre of the Maddalena lasted many years, from 1973 to the end of the 1980s. What drove us to create it? First, the awareness that in Italy women worked in theatre only as actresses, costume designers, and assistants. There were no known women directors except in a few little underground theatres. There were no known female playwrights except Franca Valeri who was relegated to the niche of variety and sketch theatre. Our theatre gave itself the task of giving space and voice to women writers, directors, musicians, and set designers. There was no discriminatory attitude toward men, who were quite welcome as audience and allies. Ours was a positive project: to give women the opportunity to speak their piece. Excluding hatred, sexual racism, and professional resistance. The Theatre of the Maddalena had a great deal of success. The biggest problems came from the contradiction between democratic politics and professionalism. Professionalism called for competition, selection, and artistic rigor. Democratic politics, on the other hand, insisted that all be equal, that all have the same opportunities. But art is not democratic. Some have talent and some don't, some have a gift for expressing

themselves and others don't. This contrast created the most difficult conflicts within the
group. On one hand, we gave space also to
those without talent, without skills, out of pure
democratic spirit. On the other hand, we real-
ized that by doing so we were dangerously
lowering the level of quality of our theatre. So
we decided to be more rigorous, but rigor gave
birth to frustration and rancor. All in all a
difficult cycle to break. Finally professionalism
won out. It was a theatrical necessity. But it cost
us so much in arguments till three in the morning, fights, insults, hurt feelings, vindictiveness
and bad humor!

B.G.: You obviously believed and probably still do
in the theatre's social function, in its being a
potent vehicle for awakening public consciousness and for exposing and exploring complex
social issues. What is it that makes the theatre
such a powerful tool for change? Is it its imme-
diacy – the dialogue, the currency of language,
plenty of action?

D.M.: True, theatre is a very powerful instrument
of social consciousness. I think this derives
from the fact that theatre was born as a religious moment. On the most ancient stages were
ritualized the difficult relations between man
and the gods, and consequently also the difficult relations between man and other men, or
between man and community. Remember that
in all the ancient Greek tragedies, the first we
know, which we love and which have entered
into our deepest mentality, there is always a

chorus that comments and judges? Theatre was the place where the community became conscious of itself, asked questions of the gods, accused itself of the gravest evils, showed pity for the weak and admiration for rebels, set the terms for living in peace with other peoples. I think that, more than the novel, theatre is the place best adapted for exploring the ethical questions of civil harmony. Even though, with the bourgeoisie, an effort was made to transform theatre into pure entertainment, or worse, into a vehicle for stupid ideas and passing fads. But the religious, ethical foundation of theatre remains no matter what.

B.G.: Was any of your work staged at the Maddalena? Which kind of plays were generally produced and who were the authors? How were the texts selected?

D.M.: Sure, many of my texts were performed at the Maddalena over the years. Among the most successful: *Suor Juana, Dialogue of a Prostitute and Her Client, Circus Bath Balò*. I directed some of them. As a general rule the texts were read in assembly. The assembly was composed of thirty or forty people. The majority decided whether to put them on or not. By spending very little and exploiting ourselves (everyone worked for free), we managed to produce five or six texts per season, which is quite a bit for a tiny little theatre company. I can remember some of the authors who had successes with the Maddalena: Adele Cambria, Mariola Boggio, Annabella Cerliani, Edith Bruck, Lù Leone, Anna Piccioni.

B.G.: Your interest in the theatre has continued into
the present. You have recently published a
theatrical monologue, *Lettere d'amore (Love
Letters)*, which is based on unpublished letters
by Gabriele D'Annunzio. Why D'Annuzio?
What attracted you to this dark romantic?

D.M.: I came upon D'Annunzio for the simple
reason that I have a house in the Abruzzo
region near the place he was born. And also
perhaps out of curiosity toward one of the most
lauded and denigrated writers of the twentieth
century, I wanted to reread him and re-evaluate
him. The "Divine Gabriele" is in effect an
egocentric and narcissistic aesthete with a great
talent for the musicality of language and very
little interest in narrative structure. His novels
are devoid of architecture but they have a
fascinating poetic fluidity. Beyond that he was
an unconscious and irreducible misogynist.
Convinced that he "loved women," he reduced
them to icons without thought or personality.
The female characters in his novels are laughable. He paid no attention to the psychology
of his characters and ethics meant nothing to
him. And yet certain descriptions of nature are
absolutely gorgeous. He had an intense sensuality for colors and odors which he expressed
in an elegant and refined choice of words. I
went to visit his house, which is lugubrious and
suffocating, stuffed with objects that recall
physical pain and agonizing death. You leave
there in anguish. His love affairs took place in
the darkness of rooms overstuffed with antique
fabrics, precious statues (though not only; in

fact, some are in the worst taste), perfume and incense. But his gardens are very beautiful, respectful of the plants; they make room for flowing water and rocks. Altogether, certainly, as you say, a livid and mortuary romanticism, recreated by an art nouveau dandy. A strange literary object, especially for Italy in that period. On the occasion of my visit I held in my hands his unedited letters written to Barbara Leoni, one of his innumerable lovers. Lovers whom he adored, courted, put on a pedestal, and then abandoned shortly thereafter, often with a child or two in the picture. Sometimes he also exploited them, as he did with Eleonora Duse, who slit her wrists over him, ignoring his infinite betrayals both sexual and professional. (Duse was a great actress; he wrote plays which he promised to her and then gave to someone else, as he did with Sarah Bernhard, because they offered a better deal.) So from these letters came the idea for a play that would use D'Annunzio's words but at the same time would introduce a character and a story that in reality had little to do with D'Annunzio.

B.G.: Not unlike your earlier work, *Insolina*, your recent collection of stories, *Buio* (*Darkness*), takes the reader along on a journey through a horror-land, places of darkness and suffering, sickness and death, all reflecting a demonic side to our social reality. Here too we enter so many "lagers" – from mysterious neurological spaces where evil hatches, transforming people into victimizers and killers, to unfeeling institutions whose mandate is to care for people but which, instead, they turn into victims. Apparently, you gathered these stories from reality, from reading "crime pages?" How was this project born? Is one of the writer's responsibilities to be a witness?

D.M.: I maintain that the writer is really a witness to her time. But far be it from me to impose a pre-established moral on the writer. There are many ways to witness your own time, and not all of them pass through the darkest zones of contemporary consciousness. It's true that in the case of *Darkness* I was inspired by the crime reports. In fact, I actually collected the stories as they were described in the newspapers. But I kept for myself the liberty to interpret them in my own way. The naked expression of the facts is true, but the way of making the characters move and speak is invented. I didn't conduct a journalistic process as I did with *Isolina,* by going to the place (in the case of *Isolina,* to Verona) to speak with people, to gather written testimony. I let my imagination construct the characters according to its own sensibility.

B.G.: I was moved by your ability to give, as it were, a human face to a material that is so repugnant. The victims in *Darkness,* like Gram, sister Attanasia or Alicetta, exude sweetness and gentleness, which make their innocence heartbreakingly poignant and consequently their demise so insufferably cruel. But even in their worlds there is some hope. The sisterhood of nuns, for instance, supports and gives comfort to Attanasia, a rape-victim, suggesting generosity in a place heavily tinted by institutionalized self-righteousness – in this case the Church. Can ugliness be transformed into beauty? Can art redeem the horrors of reality? This is one question that you often ask in your writing, don't you?

D.M.: In his own time Aristotle asked himself why a real corpse horrifies us, while an actor playing a corpse on stage can provoke immense aesthetic and ethical pleasure. Perhaps because we project onto that fictional corpse the anguish that the genuine corpse provokes in us? Perhaps because the representation of death permits us to sublimate the fear of death that we always carry with us? Perhaps because the imitation of reality gives us a way (though we know it to be illusory) of stopping time, crystallizing it and making it eternal? Probably all these things together. The fact is that representing, imitating, reconstructing reality is a way to intervene in it, even if only to make it material for reflection and contemplation. By staging suffering, we distance ourselves from it and generally from all that is too bloody and thorny, and we transform it into an object of contemplation; this gives us pleasure and often joy. Naturally, in order for the transference to work, the "means" has to be found, that is, the style of telling the story, or representing it or imitating it, must be expressive and deep; "beautiful" in Croce's words. And beauty, finally is always educative, not in a pedestrian, pedantic way, but in a way that is powerful and complex.

B.G.: In a lesser key, you speak of a divided world. The issue of "good" and "bad" taste comes up in *Bagheria* every now and then. Though you deal with it from the point of view of a young girl, your dramatized self, the impulse is to see the world in terms of refinement and kitsch-high art-low art. Has this been a continuous thought of yours, this evaluative impulse, which obviously becomes problematic when we come to judge literary production, especially the literatures of other cultures and minority groups?

D.M.: Yes, it's a problem that is complicated and not entirely clear. What does "popular art" mean? Is there an illiterate art? A wild and spontaneous art? And what is its relation to high art, sophisticated and self-aware? In many years of reflection on this question I have never come to a satisfying answer. In the 1960s, perhaps ingenuously, I believed the seductive idea that art was a product of class and therefore the great bourgeois novel, for example, necessarily had to reflect the interests of the great landowners and nascent capitalism. An art of the rich, in effect, that excluded and made ridiculous the poor. In consequence we preferred to praise the products of popular creativity, anything made by craftsmen and by hand. Preference was given to those artistic works that had not passed through the universities, but rather came from workshops, warehouses, from the fields. Work songs, protest songs, objects for daily use, primitive painting, dialect poetry, etc. But as the years went by this all began to seem schematic and unfair. When analyzing the great writers it was impossible not to recognize that they were very sensitive to the position of those who were excluded (read Dostoevski, Chekhov, Dickens). And not only that, but you had to admit that popular art was not always autonomous and independent, but rather took up, with some delay and distortion, the stylistic motifs, the discoveries, and the tastes of learned art. From this we deduced that there is no rigidly class-dependent art and that the relations between one class and another, as concerns sensibility and taste, are more profound, extensive, and unpredictable than we can imagine. So today I can only say that the whole thing is very complicated; there does certainly exist art that is ingenuous, uncultured, and popular that deserves to be taken very seriously, but that is no reason to disdain art that is sophisticated and self-aware. In sum, for one who loves it, culture will always be more free, more complex, and more mysterious than any political or historical reflection on it.

B.G.: Although your fiction is socially and politically focused, almost always grounded in phenomenal reality or taken from history, you often speak about aesthetics. In *Beloved Writing*, you maintain that "writing is a project, science, construction," which has "nothing to do with nature." There is no writing without technique, you say. What you say is similar to what our literary critic, Northrop Frye, meant with his "Ferdinand the Bull Theory of Writing" – it is not enough for a poet-to-be to smell a bunch of flowers to be able to write a sonnet. Can you expand on this apparent dichotomy between reality and representation?

D.M.: As I said before, I believe that there is "spontaneous" writing of great quality, such as for example drawings by children or the insane, such as the paintings by the Australian aborigenes (which, however, now that they've entered the international market, can no longer be called primitive), such as popular work songs or the poetry that comes from the nostalgia of a prisoner or the suffering of a worker shut up inside a factory. They have such strength that very sophisticated artists often imitate these poor forms of art and take them as models; the art of the marginalized, the anonymous art you find on the walls of public bathrooms, in the train stations, in the asylums. They add their consciousness and the culture of an artist aware of her own talent and instruments of expression.

    Spontaneous art is linked to chance, to the moment, to instinct, and is often unrepeatable, while cultured art tends to construct itself according to sign systems, self-knowledge, and technical expertise. Above all, sophisticated art quickly becomes a profession for its practitioner, with all the risks, the responsibilities, the need to evolve and the commitment that a profession calls for. From this comes the possibility, for example, to make books or music or sculptures, in effect products for widespread enjoyment (which we recognize carry the risk of commercial exploitation), products which can be taken as models and introduced into the schools and taught as sources of learning and awareness. Think of a masterpiece such as *The Odyssey,* which has crossed millennia and has never failed in its job of amazing, of making us learn, reflect, and enjoy, in addition to its themes, its stories, its rhythms, and its literary musicality.

B.G.: You often said that good writing must be sensuous. What do you mean by this?

D.M.: There is a sensuality in storytelling that consists not only in speaking of erotic themes, but in constructing a language that procures sensual pleasure in the act of reading. Language can be flat, bureaucratic, cold, sumptuous, elegant, baroque, satisfied, consolatory, aristocratic, conventional, or rather festive, joyous, hot, burlesque, ironic, lashing, musical, sensual, and so on. Sensuality comes from the wise choice of words, the carnal use of metaphors, the insistence on details from the world of the senses, the inventiveness of the descriptions.

B.G.: The fictional universe your characters occupy seems to be determined by humans – by human institutions and history, by individual desires and will to power. There seems to be no external force, no gods. Only blind faith. How would you describe your world?

D.M.: I am not a religious person. Naturally I believe that history, the long course of history, determines the path of mankind. I don't believe that there is a strategy from on high, from some

divinity who observes and determines the to-
morrows of human beings. I don't believe in a
paradise where Mother Teresa of Calcutta
walks on rose petals accompanied by a chorus
of angels, or a hell where mafiosi go naked with
lots of devils chasing after, whipping them for
the evils they committed during their lives as
criminals. Therefore I give a lot of importance
to history. I like to know it and interrogate it.
Every generation tends to give its own inter-
pretation to history. And it's thrilling how
viewpoints can change over the centuries.
Feminism, for example, was a huge effort to
reinterpret history from the point of view of
women. And it was extremely useful, beyond
its extravagances and extremism. We came to
understand that many books, including scien-
tific books, that were written with a pretense
of historical truth were completely unaware,
intentionally unaware, of the pre-established
models of the two genders. The pretense of a
male universality which included women as
well created major identity problems in
women, which still exist, and are at the base of
much misunderstanding and unhappiness. The
word Man includes women as well and aspires
to universality, while the word Women is limited to one gender only, which is often regarded
as a side-issue, peripheral, mistaken, as enemy.
We still have not escaped from anthropocen-
trism, notwithstanding all the dreams of liberty
and emancipation. In some of the richest countries things have improved, but look around,
widen your gaze a little, and you see that in
many countries women are still kept in a state

LOVE LETTERS   89

of slavery, of terror, of subjection, they get
castrated, bought and sold and even killed as
children only because they are female, as still
happens in many parts of India.

B.G.: There seems to be two forces at work in the
contemporary world-both problematic. One is
centripetal, the other centrifugal, one plural-
izes, the other globalizes. The question of frag-
mentation is of a particular interest for North
Americans. Multiculturalism, which has lately
generated heated debates in the U.S. and Canada, was originally conceived as an ideal which,
if properly carried out, would replace the
dominant vision of the world with a genuinely
pluralistic one. Those who speak disapprov-
ingly of this project see it as a pernicious, new
type of social repression. Is multiculturalism a
valid, realizable ideal or simply a recipe for
chaos? How do you see it in the Italian context?

D.M.: As often happens, wisdom resides in the
middle of the issue. The extreme fragmenta-
tion and theorizing about cultural multiplicity
leads to excesses, such as that of permitting, in
an Italian hospital, the cutting away of the
clitoris of a five year old girl at the request of
her parents, out of "respect for the traditions
of the African people." On the other hand, the
myth of globalization leads to grotesque situ-
ations such as thinking that everything can be
resolved at the click of a mouse, by provoking
to action an international network that spon-
taneously expresses the future of the world.

B.G.: Doesn't globalization have a devouring tendency towards homogeneity? Isn't there a danger that the whole world will soon turn into one big lager?

D.M.: Lager, I don't know, but conformism, yes. For anyone who travels, it is already partially underway; in every country in the world the same language is spoken: English. We eat the same things (American-style fast food), we listen to the same music, we go see the same movies (American). Local tastes and traditions are put in display cases, transformed into folklore, which is to say that they are dead, transformed into relics held up to the public like in a museum for tourists.

B.G.: Can you tell us something about your current project?

D.M.: I am working on a novel that I would rather not talk about. Until I finish it, I'll keep it to myself. But recently I have interrupted that to study an ocean of notes that my father gathered in a bunch of notebooks over many years. He was a genuine collector of words and thoughts. The notebooks are beautiful, full of pasted-in pictures, copied quotations, strange plays on words, poetry gathered here and there, scattered thoughts, sharp observations on Eastern and Western religion, etc. My father was very sick this past winter; though he's getting better now, he doesn't want to touch them. My editor asked me to turn them into a book. I don't know whether I'll manage it; it's a thankless and difficult job. My father needs money and this would help him manage. What should I do? Can filial love overcome my wise determination to cultivate my own garden?

Love Letters was born from the reexamination of a poet wildly adored in the first half of the twentieth century – during the First World War and the Fascist Era – and then reviled with equal passion in the second half. I reread his great novels but especially his poetry, rich with extraordinary sounds.

I had in hand many of his personal letters, which · remain unedited because the many women D'Annunzio loved – or at least those whom he courted and made love to – kept them jealously for themselves.

In my drama, D'Annunzio's love letters become the dark spirit of a thorny relationship between a mother and daughter. The reading of them provokes a confrontation between a living woman and a dead one who, as Pirandello might say, lived behind a strange and indecipherable mask.

Dacia Maraini